AMOROUS TURKEYS
AND
ADDICTED DUCKLINGS

A SEARCH FOR THE CAUSES OF
SOCIAL ATTACHMENT

AMOROUS TURKEYS
AND
ADDICTED DUCKLINGS
A SEARCH FOR THE CAUSES OF SOCIAL ATTACHMENT

HOWARD S. HOFFMAN

Authors Cooperative, Inc., Publishers
P. O. Box 990053
Boston, MA 02199-0053

AMOROUS TURKEYS AND ADDICTED DUCKLINGS:
A SEARCH FOR THE CAUSES OF SOCIAL ATTACHMENT.
Copyright © 1996 by Howard S. Hoffman.

For information, address:
Authors Cooperative, Inc.
Publishers
P. O. Box 990053
Boston, MA 02199-0053

ISBN 0-9623311-7-1
Library of Congress Catalogue Card Number: 95-083860

Printed in the United States of America

The stumbling way in which even the ablest of scientists in every generation have had to fight through thickets of erroneous observations, misleading generalizations, inadequate formulations, and unconscious prejudice is rarely appreciated by those who obtain their scientific knowledge from textbooks. (p. 44).

—James B Conant (1951)

Foreword

W hat has the behavior of newborn ducklings got to do with the behavior of humans? In 1932, some goslings imprinted on Konrad Lorenz and followed him on a walk. Mothers of new-borns and their doctors have been reacting ever since. Hoffman wonders if Lorenz got it right. He wants nothing less than to understand the global aspects of human behavior. Like other modern experimental scientists, he believes that the road to this goal is via the details. Understanding the big picture by studying the details has been a basic tenet of experimental natural philosophy since the 1500's when Galileo overturned fifteen hundred years of Aristotelian dogma concerning the concept of natural motion. Stephen Jay Gould makes us think about a billion years of evolution by telling us the detailed story of a few creatures. Roger Penrose tries to come to grips with the concept of consciousness by exposing us to lengthy and complicated mathematical theorems. Howard Hoffman asks us to question some modern-day dogma concerning human behavior and he does this via a detailed account of several decades of research with new-born ducklings studied under very carefully-controlled conditions. Hoffman takes us inside his lab. We can almost see ourselves cleaning the ducklings' cages and returning at 3 am to change the water. This is what real scientists do. The think/propose/experiment/analyze/rethink and start-all-over-again process is the same in experimental psychology as it is in quantum chemistry, neurobiology, or nuclear physics. We get inside a scientist who goes to work each day with an open mind and a thirst for finding out what makes us tick. We are treated to flashes of brilliance, months on the wrong path, very funny encounters (like the sneezing rat), huge disappointments, major put-downs by the "great" scientist of the day (Lorenz), the important role of serendipity, and the thrill of thinking you understand some aspect of mammalian behavior just a little bit better at the end of the day.

How do you respond to a crying child? Is there a critical bonding period after birth? There are too many books and papers that prove the correctness of one extreme answer for issues like these. There are also too many books and papers that prove the correctness of the opposite extreme answer. Hoffman tries to help us understand the slowly evolving maxim that there are only two kinds of theories: wrong ones and those that aren't yet proven wrong. How do we relate to those we love deeply? Does familiarity breed contempt? Does absence make the heart grow fonder? Does our social and physical environment shape our actions more than our genetic makeup? Are we genetically predisposed to violence, as Desmond Morris would have it, or not, as Richard Leakey would have it? Are our interactions with our environment algorithmic? Are we the sum of our parts or is this 3000 year-old philosophy not quite right as the non-linear dynamicists would suggest? Are we all on drugs most of the time because that's how our brain and body work? What does the combination of an open mind and decades of research with the behavior of ducklings in the laboratory say about how these matters relate to human behavior? Hoffman would like the reader to come to her own conclusions.

Books that use the physical sciences as their backdrop to teach the big picture fail to reach most educated readers because the underpinnings are either too difficult or the concepts too exotic. The backdrop here is ducklings wandering around cages. You don't have to be a rocket scientist to understand the real science in this book. It will appeal to the student of experimental psychology who wants to see how it is done and it will appeal to the rest of us who are curious about what makes us tick.

Peter Beckman
Professor of Physics
Bryn Mawr College

Acknowledgments

No worthy research is ever accomplished in an intellectual vacuum. I thank the many graduate and undergraduate students who over the years participated in the work and made substantial contributions to its concepts and content. Our research was truly a cooperative enterprise. The names of these former students appear as the coauthors or sole authors of the publications from my laboratory that are cited in the text and listed among the references. I also thank Doris McCoulough for her help in typing the earliest draft of this manuscript.

I owe a special debt to Patrick Bateson, the Provost of Kings College and Professor of Ethology at Cambridge University, and to Gabriel Horn, the Head of the Department of Zoology and Master of Sidney Sussex College at Cambridge. They arranged for my stay at the University and made sure that I would have access to the facilities I would need to complete this book. I especially appreciate the insights I gained from my visits to their laboratories and from my discussions with them.

Johan Bolhuis read an early draft of the manuscript and provided a helpful critique. My many discussions with him were an important source for the sense of comradeship and shared enthusiasms of the scientific enterprise that I encountered at

Cambridge. I also want to thank Eric Keverne for seeking me out and informing me of his research at the animal behavior laboratories in the Madingley facility of Cambridge University. To learn of those findings has strengthened my confidence in the proposition that attachment is best described as a form of addictive behavior.

I am fortunate that two American colleagues have read and constructively reviewed this book. Professor Peter Beckman teaches physics at Bryn Mawr College. At the time that he offered to look at what I had written, I had become discouraged about the book ever going to press. Several major publishers had reviewed the manuscript and while each had been complimentary, none felt that they would be able to market it. Peter's enthusiasm for the book's message about the nature of research and his suggestions for how better to deliver that message provided me with the incentive to send a revised version of the manuscript to one more publisher. Although I did not realize it at the time, this meant that another colleague, Murray Sidman, would serve as editor. His expertise in behavior analysis along with his writing skills have helped me clarify both my thoughts and my writing. I know that had anyone else served as its editor, this book would have been much the less.

I owe a great debt to my wife, Alice. Besides being the source of my endorphins, she has consistently encouraged me to proceed with this book and has reviewed its account critically as it developed. In doing so, she helped me to better organize my thoughts about the work and to recognize its importance. I also want to thank my son, Daniel Hoffman, for preparing all the graphic illustrations. I could not have done so myself because I lacked the skill in computer graphics that he willingly supplied. I must add that while I am grateful for the assistance of my family and colleagues, any errors are of course mine and mine alone.

Finally, I express my appreciation to The National Institute of Mental Health. Except for the first year or so when I was just getting started, my research on imprinting was continuously supported by NIMH Grant 19715.

Howard S. Hoffman
Professor Emeritus
of Psychology
Bryn Mawr College

Contents

Contents

Introduction

This is an account of a sequence of investigations by myself and my students into the social bond that develops between an immature organism and its mother. In technical terms, the research focused on a process that Konrad Lorenz (1937) dubbed "imprinting." Young organisms were understood to be permanently affected by early experiences that occurred within a so-called "critical period."

The Lorenzian view of this process and its behavioral aftereffects has had a potent influence on the way we deal with children and with each other. It has colored the debate over the relative importance of nature versus nurture and has fostered a rigid rather than a plastic view of the biological and social environment.

Our work led us to conclude that unlike the position postulated by Lorenz and his followers, imprinting is neither rapid nor irreversible. Nor, for that matter, is imprinting limited to a brief critical period early in life, as their observations implied. Instead, our findings (along with those of certain others) led to the unexpected conclusion that imprinting is a form of gradual learning that entails an addictive process mediated by the release of endorphins (the brain's own opiates). These insights help to explain a number of otherwise puzzling observations about imprinting, including its relation to eating and to certain acts of aggression.

The conclusion that imprinting entails an addictive process has a number of practical implications. For example, the prevailing view of the way social attachment occurs determines private and public practices with respect to child care and adoption. This book represents an effort to counter the influence of the Lorenzian interpretation of imprinting by providing some of the scientific evidence against it. It is important to observe at the outset, however, that our research does not contradict the observations made by Lorenz and others. Rather, our carefully controlled laboratory experiments demonstrate that there are better explanations for the behavior that Lorenz and his colleagues observed in their studies of animals in their natural surroundings.

I have sought here to describe our experiments in terms that would convey their essential implications understandably and convincingly to the nospecialist. I have also tried to provide readers, especially budding scientists, with some of the flavor of our research projects. Information about what happens behind the scenes in a busy laboratory is seldom available to nonspecialists.

Detailed descriptions of research findings are, of course, available in the original research reports and we often find summaries in newspapers, magazines or textbooks. But most of these sources are bloodless; they fail to convey what research is really like. Textbooks and other secondary sources usually oversimplify research, glossing over its details and controversial aspects. Good scientific reports always include reasonably detailed descriptions of how things were done and attempt to deal with the controversial aspects of the work, but such reports rarely elaborate the sometimes mundane problems that had to be resolved before the research could move forward. Nor do they include within their pages the irony, serendipity, and occasional humor that give life to a project and make science a human enterprise. I wanted, in this volume, to provide some of that information.

Finally, I wanted to describe how the findings from our laboratory fit with the work of other contemporary investigators. Our research on imprinting spanned a 15-year interval that ended in the early 1980's. In the past dozen years, after the work in my laboratory had turned to other issues, much seminal research on imprinting was accomplished, especially in England and Holland. The later chapters of this volume are devoted to an examination of that research and its relations to the work we had done.

1

Getting Started

When Lorenz coined the term "imprinting," he used it to describe the process by which greylag goslings come to be socially bonded to whatever moving object they first encounter. He observed that if exposed to a human being during the first few hours after hatching, the goslings became socially attached to the human in much the same fashion as they would ordinarily become socially attached to their natural mother. The process seemed to occur so rapidly that it appeared as if the image of the human had been instantly and indelibly imprinted on the gosling's nervous system. Lorenz illustrated the strength of the resulting attachment with a now classic photograph of a half dozen or so goslings following him in a line.

The Tale of the Amorous Turkeys

In the early 1960's, when my own work on imprinting began, I was familiar with Lorenz's observations and with his interpretations of them. I was also aware that there was much more to be learned about imprinting and that such work might provide important insights into the basic processes that are responsible for social attachments. At the time, however, I was working on a variety of issues, none directly related to social attachment. My special interest in imprinting was largely a product of two fortuitous events. The first of these occurred in the course of a series of informal bag lunch seminars among certain members of the psychology, biology, and animal husbandry departments at the Pennsylvania State University. At the time, I was a new assistant professor trained as an experimental psychologist at the University of Connecticut. I had learned to ask questions about why we act as we do and to carry out experiments that would help answer these questions by yielding data that anyone could examine and evaluate. I had also learned that many aspects of human biology and behavior are mirrored in the biology and behavior of other species. Because they dealt with many different species, the bag lunches provided a unique opportunity for me to learn about the biology and behavior of organisms that psychologists seldom study.

At one of the bag lunches I learned of research that Edgar Hale and Martin Schein were conducting at the Penn State Poultry Farm. These investigators were studying the courtship behavior of turkeys, a topic that was of considerable interest to farmers whose livelihood depended on the successful breeding of these birds. In the course of our seminars I came to be friends with Hale and Schein, and one evening, while working in my office, I received a telephone call from Schein. As I recall, he simply asked me to come over to his laboratory. He had something interesting to show me.

When I arrived, I was escorted down a dimly lit corridor that ended with two doors leading to adjacent experimental rooms. Each door contained a one-way vision window, designed to enable an experimenter to observe what was transpiring within a room without being observed by the room's occupants. In this instance, the occupants of both rooms were turkeys. They were full grown males and there were about 35 of them in each room. As we stood in the hall, I was told to study the birds in the two rooms to see if I could detect any differences between them. I examined them through the windows as best I could, but I could see no differences that amounted to anything. The birds in both rooms were about the same size, had the same physical appearance, and seemed to be behaving in the same way. In short, they looked like two ordinary flocks of turkeys.

What happened over the next few minutes, however, made it clear that the birds in one of these rooms were anything but ordinary. First, I was invited to enter the nearest of the rooms. As soon as I opened the door the birds fled to the furthest corner. Furthermore, whenever I walked toward them, they would slide along the wall in such a way as to maintain the maximum distance between me and them. There was no question about it; these birds were avoiding me. I was told that the birds in the room I had entered first were members of a control group. They had been hatched in a normal fashion and had not had much previous contact with humans.

Next, I was told to go into the second room. I did so and, to my amazement, these birds behaved entirely differently. Instead of fleeing, they stopped dead in their tracks, fixed their gaze on me, and went into a full courtship strut. When a turkey is exhibiting courtship behavior, its tail spreads into a broad fan, its head draws back, and its wattles (the red fleshy protuberances that hang below its throat) grow in length. Each of the birds did all of these things. Not only that: every single one of them began to move toward me in the slow ponderous way of a turkey intent on copulation. Needless to say, I fled. This was, I should mention, no difficult feat; anyone who has watched a tom turkey during courtship knows that its motions are excruciatingly slow. This observation alone may help to explain the need for research on this topic.

What Hale and Schein had been studying was the effect of the male hormone, testosterone, on the behavior of newly hatched turkey poults (Schein and Hale, 1959). Testosterone appears to be responsible for courtship behavior in the adult male of many species. Among other things, Schein and Hale wanted to find out whether injections of testosterone would induce immature males to display adult type courtship behavior. They also wanted to determine what kinds of stimuli might elicit this behavior. They had found that when injected, a young male will indeed engage in a full strut, and will direct this behavior mostly toward the investigators who administer the injection.

The birds in the second room were these experimental subjects, now fully grown. I was told that these birds would sometimes react positively to female turkeys, but that their response was uncertain. Humans, on the other hand, could reliably elicit a courtship response, as I had done as soon as I entered their room. Apparently as a result of their exposure to humans when they were receiving testosterone, these birds developed a sexual preference for humans. When the experiment ended, and they no longer were being injected, they stopped exhibiting courtship behavior altogether and reacted to humans much like other turkeys at their age. Later, however, when they were older and were producing their own testosterone, they began again to display courtship behavior when they encountered a human.

I have always thought that this pattern of results suggests that for turkeys and perhaps other organisms as well, sexual preferences may depend on the kind of stimulation encountered during the period of development when the body begins to produce sex hormones in large amounts. Clearly, however, the issue is speculative and would require direct investigation before it could be resolved satisfactorily. The point is that this curious incident provided me with an important lesson. It served as an unforgettable example of the powerful and enduring behavioral effects that can be engendered by certain kinds of early experiences.

Extending the Domain of Imprinting

The second event that prompted me to work in the domain of imprinting was a paper by Neil Peterson (1960), who at the time was a graduate student in B. F. Skinner's laboratory at Harvard. Peterson reported an experiment in which he trained newly hatched ducklings to peck at a small target by arranging for each peck to provide the bird with a brief glimpse of a moving inanimate object to which it had been imprinted previously.

Peterson's paper was of special interest to me for several reasons. First, I considered it an extraordinarily creative study. It convincingly demonstrated that, like the presentation of food to a hungry rat, the mere sight of an imprinting stimulus—an object to which a duckling had become imprinted—can reinforce the actions of that subject. Second, it suggested a way to study the infant/mother bond while avoiding some of the pitfalls that ordinarily accompany research of this type. In most social relationships, and especially in the bond between an infant and its mother, there is a reciprocal effect: the behavior of each member of the pair is at least in part a reaction to the other member. This factor can greatly complicate studies of social relationships because it means that procedures that might influence one member of a social pair may (via that member's reaction) also affect the other member. Peterson's paper showed me how I might circumvent this problem by using the imprinting phenomenon to establish an infant duckling's reaction to a "parent" that was an inanimate object. The behavior of the object (the "parent") could then be placed under the experimenter's control, and its relation to the behavior of the duckling could be determined completely by the requirements of the particular issue under investigation.

I might comment in this regard that although the subjects in our research were always ducklings, the focus of our interest was never ducklings per se. We viewed our subjects as a means to an understanding of social bonding in general. That we were testing ducklings was more a matter of experimental expedience than anything else. This is not to say that we did not find our ducklings interesting and at times appealing. On the contrary, I and my students were fascinated by the behavior of our young subjects and we even became fond of them. But I do not think any of us would have pursued this line of investigation if we thought that it was only going to tell us something about ducklings.

I came to this work with the orientation of an experimental psychologist. A fundamental assumption of most experimental psychologists is that nature has great continuity and that if a behavioral process is observed in lower organisms, there is a good chance that it will also operate in higher organisms. This explains why experimental psychologists are as likely to be found studying the behavior of rats, pigeons, or primates as the behavior of humans. This is not to suggest that I or any other experimental psychologist believe that a given kind of behavior is likely to be identical across species. On the contrary, we all know that each species displays its own specialized physical characteristics and that its behavior can be just as unique as its appearance. We also know, however, that developments in nature are usually gradual and cumulative. What may seem to be unique behavior in higher organisms often turns out to be an elaboration of simpler behavior that we see in a lower animal. When I first undertook to study imprinting, I hoped that social bonding in humans might prove to be an elaboration of the same behavioral processes that I planned to study in ducklings. As will be seen in later chapters, the evidence is clear that this is exactly what happened.

Practical, Mundane Aspects of Research

Once I decided to study imprinting, it was necessary to make certain preparations. For one thing, my students and I needed to construct housing for the ducklings. For another, we needed to build and test the apparatus that would be used. As often happens in science, one of these seemingly mundane tasks (housing the ducks) posed major problems.

After inquiring in a number of places, I eventually learned of a farm in Ohio that would ship day-old fertilized duck eggs. I ordered several dozen, and Marty Schein set aside some space in his incubator.

Duck eggs take 28 days to hatch. My students and I used this time to build several chambers in which to imprint and train ducklings. These chambers were modeled after the imprinting unit developed by Peterson. Like his, they were designed to provide a well controlled setting in which we could imprint our ducklings and train them to peck at a target. At first we constructed two units, but for later studies we built four more. Each consisted of a six-foot long plywood box divided by a fine mesh stainless steel screen into two equal sized compartments, one for the duckling and the other for the stimulus to which the duckling was to be imprinted.

For some of our initial work, the imprinting stimulus consisted of a white plastic milk bottle mounted over the engine of a model electric train. Later, because plastic milk bottles were hard to find, we simply covered the engine with a rectangular block of foam rubber. Special electronic equipment was used to control this engine so that when programmed to do so, it would move back and forth on its track along the length of its compartment at a rate of about a foot per second.

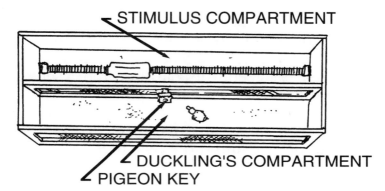

STIMULUS COMPARTMENT

DUCKLING'S COMPARTMENT
PIGEON KEY

Figure 1. Top view of the apparatus for imprinting and key-peck training.

Figure 1 shows a top view of one of our units. A number of incandescent lamps were mounted above the screen in each compartment. The lamps in the subject's compartment were lit continuously and were focused so that they produced reflections on the screen that prevented the subject from seeing into the stimulus compartment unless the lamps in that compartment were also illuminated. With this arrangement, presentation of the imprinting stimulus required only that we illuminate the stimulus compartment and send power to the engine.

In our early studies, we taught our ducklings to peck at a target by reinforcing this behavior with a brief opportunity to view the moving imprinting stimulus. For this work, the target for the duckling's pecks was a translucent plastic paddle that was fastened to a sensitive switch and mounted in a small metal container with a circular opening in the front (see Figures 1 and 2). This target had first been used in experiments with pigeons as subjects; hence, it is called a pigeon key. For some of our later studies we stopped using a pigeon key as the target and replaced it with a lightweight balsa wood pole that was mounted vertically in a recessed slot in the center of the stainless steel screen. The pole hung from a sensitive switch that was wired into the programming equipment so that pecks at the pole (as had pecks at the pigeon key) would cause a brief stimulus presentation. We found the pole preferable to the pigeon key because it could accommodate ducklings of any size without our having to adjust its height.

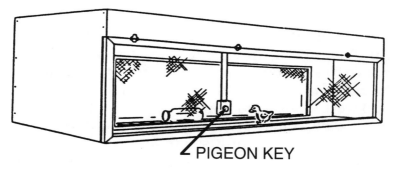

PIGEON KEY

Figure 2. Experimenter's view of the apparatus for imprinting and key peck training. As shown here, the far compartment has been illuminated and power has been delivered to the engine. The duckling is therefore able to see (and hear) the imprinting stimulus (the milk bottle) as it moves back and forth along its tracks.

We also constructed what we thought would be appropriate housing units for ducklings. These units consisted of banks of 24 individual wooden brooder boxes with wire mesh floors. Each box was about ten inches on a side and contained a 40-watt light bulb to supply heat and illumination.

The idea was that when in these boxes, the ducklings might be able to hear each other but would be visually isolated. We had modeled the boxes after the brooder units that Hale and Schein had used to house their turkey poults. As it turned out, this was a mistake.

We had failed to take into account the fact that the digestive system of a duckling differs from that of a turkey. Perhaps because it is an aquatic bird, a duckling's fecal matter has a loose consistency initially, but when it dries, it forms a rocklike mass that sticks tenaciously to any surface it contacts. As a result, we found it almost impossible to maintain their housing units in a sanitary condition. Another problem that we had failed to anticipate was how rapidly ducklings grow. Within a week of their arrival it was clear that even if we found a way to clean their housing units effectively, the birds would outgrow them in just a few days.

I was very discouraged by these problems and had they persisted, I might have abandoned all work on imprinting. Fortunately, however, both problems were quickly solved in a surprisingly simple fashion. After considering disposable housing units, it occurred to me that I really did not need to replace whole units. All I really needed were disposable linings that could be inserted into permanent units.

After trying various kinds of units, we purchased a number of 15-gallon white translucent plastic food containers of the sort used by large restaurants. (Experimental psychologists are always ready to adapt technically sophisticated equipment from other areas). Each container was lined with a heavy-duty transparent plastic bag, and an inch or so of Sanicel was spread across its bottom to form a smooth floor. Sanicel is a commercial bedding material that provided solid footing for the birds and also tended to absorb their droppings. In these units, food and water were continuously available from disposable plastic cups that were held by a wire support inside the bag.

This system proved to be very nearly ideal for our purposes. The containers kept the birds in visual isolation and yet admitted enough light to insure normal visual development. Moreover, the units were big enough to accommodate the ducklings until they were almost fully grown. We also found it easy and inexpensive to maintain the units in a sanitary condition. To do so required only that the plastic bag and its contents be replaced as needed.

2

The Early Studies

In many respects, the history of science is as much the story of the correction of wrong conclusions as it is an account of major breakthroughs and brilliant deductions. Perhaps this is obvious. After all, for almost any set of observations or findings, there are likely to be many ways to make wrong conclusions but only one way to be right. I mention this because our earliest experiments on imprinting led us to some wrong conclusions. Those conclusions seemed irrefutable at the time and I will explain why. Before doing so, however, I need to describe some of the events that occurred during that early work.

Imprinting and Reinforcement

Peterson had shown that the presentation of a stimulus to which a duckling had been imprinted could reinforce the duckling's tendency to peck a target. His study had not, however, addressed the issue of whether or not prior imprinting was, in fact, necessary for this effect. It seemed possible that something about the sight of an appropriate imprinting stimulus might be intrinsically reinforcing to a young duckling. If this were so, then the prior imprinting in Peterson's experiment would have been superfluous. This possibility in no way detracted from my admiration of Peterson's groundbreaking work but it raised the question of whether or not his results were, in fact, relevant to social bonding. Our first study was designed to answer this question. The idea was to repeat Peterson's basic experiment while adding a number of control groups. Before describing the conditions for those groups, however, I need to describe the way Peterson trained his birds to peck the target.

The procedure that Peterson used is called response shaping. My students and I were familiar with this procedure, as we had previously used it to teach pigeons to peck at a key that was mounted on the wall of their test chamber. First, we deprived the pigeons of grain for about a day. This ensured that they would be well motivated. We then placed one of the birds in the test chamber and carefully observed its behavior. The idea was that we would drop some grain into a small hopper on the side of the chamber whenever the bird exhibited an act that was part of the behavior required to peck the key. At first, we gave the bird grain whenever it faced the key. The effect was an increase in its tendency to turn in the direction of the key as soon as it finished consuming grain. Once this behavior was occurring consistently, we withheld the delivery of grain until the bird touched or almost touched the key with its beak.

This procedure, sometimes called the method of approximation, takes a certain amount of skill on the part of the investigator, but by gradually increasing the requirement for the presentation of reinforcement (in this instance, delivery of grain), a pigeon could be rapidly induced to place its beak closer and closer to the key. Eventually, it was only necessary to wait until the bird spontaneously pecked at the key itself. This seldom took long because most birds exhibited a strong tendency to peck at the key once they had placed their beak near it. After the bird pecked for the first time, we discontinued the shaping procedure and handed the control over food delivery to the bird itself. We accomplished this by arranging that whenever a peck to the key closed its sensitive switch, a small amount of grain would be delivered automatically by an electrically operated feeding device.

The shaping procedure that Peterson used was basically the same as the one my students and I had used to train pigeons. The only essential difference was that instead of using food, Peterson gave the duckling a brief glimpse of an imprinting stimulus when its responses approximated a key peck. The fact that all of his birds learned to peck the key indicated that presenting an imprinting stimulus was an effective reinforcer. Our question, however, was whether or not this reinforcement effect depended on prior imprinting procedures.

Lorenz (1935) had found that unless goslings were exposed to a stimulus during approximately the first two days of hatching they did not form a social bond with it. Lorenz called this early interval "the critical period for imprinting." We hypothesized that if the reinforcement effect reported by Peterson was a product of imprinting, then it must have been derived from events that transpired during this critical period. Our experiment examined this proposition by conducting some variations of the basic procedure that Peterson had used. In particular, we wanted to know what would happen if ducklings received their first exposure to the imprinting stimulus long after the critical period had passed.

Ducklings in one group were individually exposed to the same imprinting procedures that Peterson had used. Within 48 hours of hatching, each bird received six 45-minute sessions in which a stimulus was continuously visible and moving. Ducklings in a second group were also individually exposed to the imprinting apparatus for six 45-minute sessions within 48 hours of hatching, but for them, the illuminated stimulus compartment was empty, the stimulus having been removed. At the conclusion of these initial sessions the birds were returned to their individual housing units where they remained for a week. Each was then given two days of training to peck at the key.

For subjects in the first group, the stimulus to which they had been exposed earlier was presented for a second or so whenever the duckling approached the key. Once the bird was in the vicinity of the key, however, only pecking-type motions and head positions near the key yielded stimulus presentation. When the duckling finally pecked the key, the imprinting stimulus was automatically presented for five seconds and any subsequent pecks at the key also yielded a five-second stimulus presentation.

For subjects in the second group—the birds that previously had been exposed to the empty stimulus compartment—two kinds of key-peck training procedures were tried. With one procedure, we presented the imprinting stimulus when the bird's behavior approximated a key peck. This was the first time these birds had seen the stimulus. With the other procedure, we presented only the empty stimulus compartment (by turning on its light) when the bird's behavior approximated a key peck.

The results of this experiment can be summarized quite simply. Every duckling in the group that had been exposed to the stimulus during the critical period for imprinting (within 48 hours of hatching) learned to peck at the key. None of the ducklings in the other group could be taught to do so.

These results were in complete accord with Peterson's findings. They indicated that, when ducklings have previously been exposed to a stimulus during the critical period, the presentation of that stimulus is adequate reinforcement for shaping and maintaining a duckling's tendency to peck at a key. They extended Peterson's findings, however, by demonstrating that once imprinting has occurred, the reinforcing effects of stimulus presentation are maintained over at least a week-long interval during which the duckling has no contact with the stimulus.

Our results also extended Peterson's findings in another way. We had found that when the initial exposure to the imprinting stimulus occurred after the critical period, we were totally unable to train any of our birds to peck the key. Our failure to train these birds to peck the key, despite what we considered to be a valiant effort, led us to conclude that reinforcing effects like those observed by Peterson and by us could only have come about as a product of earlier imprinting. In our paper (Hoffman, Searle, Toffee, and Kozma, 1966), we put it this way:

> Our findings indicate that the capacity of an imprinted stimulus to serve as a reinforcement derives from events that occur during the critical period for imprinting. (p. 188).

I think most readers will agree that this conclusion clearly follows from our results. The problem is that it is wrong. Of course, we did not know this at the time, and several years and some singular events would have to occur before we were to learn why. A hint of future developments lay in some observations we neglected at the time. We had observed that when exposed to an imprinting stimulus during the critical period, most ducklings immediately tried to follow the stimulus as it moved back and forth in its compartment. When our birds were first exposed to the imprinting stimulus after the critical period, however, their immediate reaction was to flee rather than follow the stimulus. Only later were we to recognize the significance of the immediacy of these withdrawal responses.

Still, our work had two important effects. First, it taught us that we could adequately house ducklings—a critical technical point. Second, it revealed that, like Peterson, we could train ducklings to peck at a key if we used as the sole reinforcing event the presentation of a stimulus to which they had been imprinted. This not only provided us with an investigative technique but also, as we shall see, introduced us to some questions that had not yet been asked about imprinting.

Response Patterns

Our next step was to try to determine the pattern of attachment behavior that would emerge if birds had unlimited access to an imprinting stimulus via a key peck. Several birds that had been successfully trained to peck the key (the birds that had received their initial exposure to the imprinting stimulus within 48 hours of hatching) were individually tested in a single long session.

Figure 3 shows the instrument that we used to document the ducklings' key pecks during this session, and Figure 4 shows the details of the key pecks that were documented on the torn-off section of the recording illustrated in Figure 3. During this

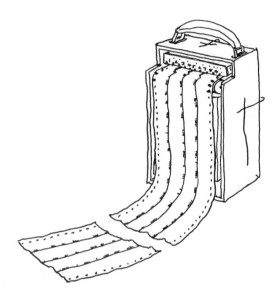

Figure 3. The 20-pen operations recorder used to document events in a given study. The recorder is shown as it simultaneously documents the key pecks of three ducklings (each in its own apparatus) when each peck yields a five-second view of the imprinting stimulus. In other experiments, one or another of the recorder's pens was used to record other events: presentations of the imprinting stimulus, distress calls, and occurrences of eating or drinking. The paper moves continuously at a predetermined rate, while the beginning and ending of a given kind of event (for example, a key peck) causes the appropriate pen to move quickly upward about an eighth of an inch and then back to its resting position. Thus, the track of a given pen leaves a permanent record of exactly when each event occurred and how long it lasted.

session, whenever the bird pecked during stimulus withdrawal it produced the stimulus briefly. If the bird pecked during a stimulus presentation, however, it did not prolong that presentation. In the session documented in Figure 4, each stimulus presentation lasted five seconds. In other experiments, different stimulus durations were sometimes used but otherwise, the same arrangement always prevailed: pecks during stimulus absence produced the stimulus for some fixed amount of time; pecks during stimulus presentation were always without effect (and were rarely observed). For this reason, rather than reflecting single long stimulus presentations, each of the solid appearing bars in Figure 4 (and in all subsequent records of key pecks) indicate a period when a duckling consistently pecked the key within a few seconds of each stimulus withdrawal.

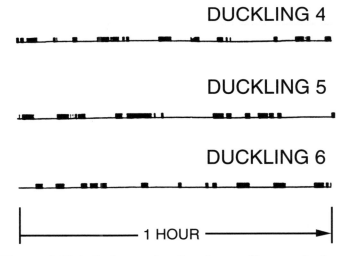

DUCKLING 4

DUCKLING 5

DUCKLING 6

|———————— 1 HOUR ————————▶|

Figure 4. Detailed records of an hour of key pecks by each of three ducklings that were being simultaneously observed in separate rooms. For these birds, each peck was reinforced with a five-second presentation of the imprinting stimulus.

24

These records document a duckling's pecks at a key when the only consequence of pecking was a brief opportunity to look at a white plastic milk bottle mounted over the cab of a moving electric train. That a duckling should peck at all in these circumstances seemed surprising. That it should peck so persistently astonished us.

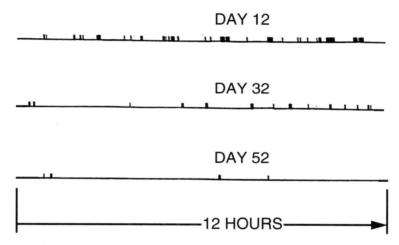

Figure 5. Sample 12-hour records of key pecks from Subject C during the 12th, 32nd, and 52nd day from hatch. Throughout this period, each key peck yielded a 15-second exposure of the imprinting stimulus.

The records in Figure 5 provided further evidence of the persistence of the duckling's efforts to view a stimulus to which it had been exposed soon after hatching. They show the pattern of pecks when a duckling was allowed to spend 24 hours per day in the imprinting apparatus for about two months. From the time the bird was first placed in the apparatus, it had continuous access to food and water and it could view the stimulus for 15 seconds whenever it pecked the key. We tested several birds

(Hoffman and Kozma, 1967) and they all behaved the same way. At first, they kept the stimulus in view for an average of slightly more than two hours per day. By the time they were two months old, however, they only pecked enough to keep the stimulus visible for an average of slightly less than 10 minutes per day. By this time, they were fully grown and fully feathered and their voices had changed. Now they quacked rather than peeped.

We were encouraged by these results. The birds' persistent pecking was good evidence that we were studying something that, to the ducklings at least, was quite important. We were puzzled, however, by one aspect of these findings. As Figures 4 and 5 showed, the birds seemed always to peck in bursts that were separated by longer intervals without pecks. At first, we thought this might just be the way that random data bunch up. When we analyzed the records statistically, however, we found that the bursts were not mere chance occurrences. If the probability of a peck were constant in time, one would expect some bunching, but the probability of a peck in a small (30-second) interval should be the same regardless of whether or not the bird had pecked in the preceding small interval of time. When, however, we painstakingly divided the records into 30-second intervals and actually assessed these probabilities, it turned out that the likelihood of a peck during a given interval was much higher if the bird had pecked in the preceding interval than if it had failed to do so (the probabilities were 0.73 and 0.29 respectively).

We wondered what might be responsible for this curious pattern of responses, but when we analyzed the records in various ways, we found nothing that seemed to cast much light on the issue. We thought, for example that the bursts of pecking for the stimulus to which a bird had been imprinted might be analogous to the bursts of eating that occur when an animal has free access to food. Within limits, the longer an animal goes without food, the more it eats. We wondered if a duckling's tendency to seek an imprinting stimulus might not work the same way. We thought that if it did, we ought to observe longer bursts after longer absences. A careful analysis of the data, however, made it clear that there was no such relation. We also examined a variety of other potential relations in the data but nothing we looked at provided any clarification. The ducklings pecked in bursts and we simply did not know why.

We did eventually learn the reason for this consistent pattern of behavior but, like our earlier erroneous conclusions with respect to the critical period, it would take several years before we would discover what was really going on. In the meantime, an incident occurred that deserves mention.

One day, when our research seemed to be progressing nicely, I was called into my department chairman's office. When I arrived he said something like the following: "Howard, What in the world is going on in your lab? Today at lunch the Dean asked me why Hoffman was constantly sending through purchase orders for electric trains."

I remember wanting to tell him to explain to the Dean that Hoffman had six kids and that Christmas was coming. I did not do that, however. As I recall, I merely described our research and suggested that he tell the Dean about it. Suffice it to say, I never again heard about any objections from the Dean to my purchases of electric trains. I have always suspected, though, that this Dean must have been convinced that psychologists are a strange lot.

3

Ducklings in Distress

I n the course of our initial efforts to shape the
key peck, we observed that ducklings often
emitted a stream of high-pitched, peep-like
vocalizations during the intervals when the
imprinting stimulus was withdrawn. Because these
sounds also occur when a duckling is hungry, cold,
or in pain, they are thought to reflect an autonomic
response to aversive conditions. For this reason,
they have been identified as distress calls (Hafez,
1958).

Measuring Distress Calls

When we measured the distress calls of newly
hatched ducklings, we found them to be relatively
intense. Moreover, the calls had a restricted
frequency range of approximately 3000 to 4000
cycles per second. (Middle C on the piano is 256
cycles per second and most pianos go up to about
4000 cycles per second.) Using this information,
we designed and built a specialized electronic unit
that would selectively respond to sounds of these
frequencies but not to other sounds. Because the
device automatically closed an electrical switch (a
relay) each time it detected a distress note, we were

able to obtain detailed records of the distress calls of individual ducklings in a variety of experimental circumstances.

In Figure 6, the top line in each duckling's record shows the pattern of distress calls recorded by this unit when the imprinting stimulus was presented and withdrawn repeatedly. The bottom line in each record shows when the stimulus was present and absent. The ducklings were about five days old and had had about two hours of exposure to the imprinting stimulus during the first 48 hours after hatching.

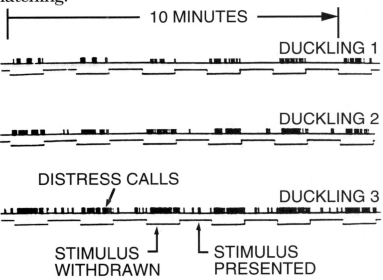

Figure 6. Distress calling during periodic presentation and withdrawal of an imprinting stimulus. Before this session, each duckling had received extended exposure to the imprinting stimulus.

My students and I were delighted by the way our new instrument worked. It proved sensitive and reliable, providing a detailed yet readily understood record of our subject's spontaneous vocal reactions.

Moreover, it did so in an objective and readily quantifiable way. It seemed to us that this instrument was likely to prove especially useful and we looked forward to what we would learn when we analyzed the records it produced.

The first thing we noticed was that the ducklings usually ceased their distress calls immediately upon each stimulus presentation, but several seconds usually elapsed before they started their distress calls again after stimulus withdrawal.

There was, of course, a certain amount of variation among individuals but overall, stimulus presentation and withdrawal were producing a profound effect on the behavior of our young subjects. Indeed, the control over distress calls that the imprinting stimulus exerted was as close to absolute as any behavioral effect we had previously encountered. Now, however, the control seemed backwards. In most laboratory studies, it is stimulus presentation that elicits a response. Here, on the other hand, the response (distress calls) was a reaction to stimulus withdrawal, and stimulus presentation terminated the response.

In one study (Hoffman, Stratton, Newby, and Barrett, 1970), we asked, "When during a duckling's exposure to an imprinting stimulus does the stimulus begin to exert this control over distress calls?" For example, must the birds have had experience with the imprinting stimulus before that stimulus will alleviate their distress? To help answer this question, we carefully monitored the incubation process, and when inspection of a given egg first revealed the pip marks that indicated a duckling was about to emerge, we placed the egg in a small metal box with holes along the top and bottom to provide ventilation. When the duckling left its shell, it emerged into the box and remained there undisturbed until the tests began.

Approximately 17 hours after the duckling was free of its shell, we quickly transferred the unopened box (containing the duckling and the remnants of its shell) from the incubator to the center of the subject compartment. Using a long string and a pulley system, we remotely lifted the box from its detachable floor. Thus, except for its experience within the box, the duckling's first visual stimulation occurred when the box was lifted. Figure 7 shows this arrangement.

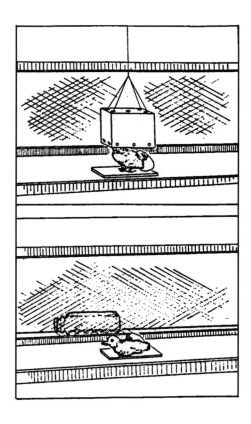

For several ducklings, the stimulus to which they were to be imprinted was presented a few seconds before the box was lifted and remained visible for one minute. For the other ducklings, the imprinting stimulus was first made visible one minute after the box was lifted. Thereafter, stimulus presentations and withdrawals occurred at 20-second intervals for both groups. The basic difference between the two groups of ducklings was whether they could see the imprinting stimulus immediately when the box was lifted, or not until one minute later.

The upper portion of Figure 8 shows the distress calls for several ducklings that saw only the subject compartment—no imprinting stimulus—when the box was lifted. The birds in this condition began their distress calls when first exposed to the apparatus—when the box was lifted—but in most instances, they ceased their distress calls almost immediately when the imprinting stimulus appeared for the first time. With subsequent withdrawals of the imprinting stimulus, distress calls typically began within two to five seconds. In general, however, the ducklings stopped their distress calls within one second after the imprinting stimulus became visible again.

The lower portion of Figure 8 shows records obtained from birds that could see the imprinting stimulus immediately upon the lifting of the hatch

---

Figure 7. The top drawing shows the removal of the hatching box from a 17-hour-old duckling when the imprinting stimulus was not present. The bottom drawing shows the same duckling during the initial stimulus presentation. In both drawings, the object beside the duckling is the remnant of its shell.

box. These ducklings made no distress calls until the stimulus was first withdrawn. Thereafter, however, they exhibited the same pattern of calls as the birds represented in the upper portion of Figure 8.

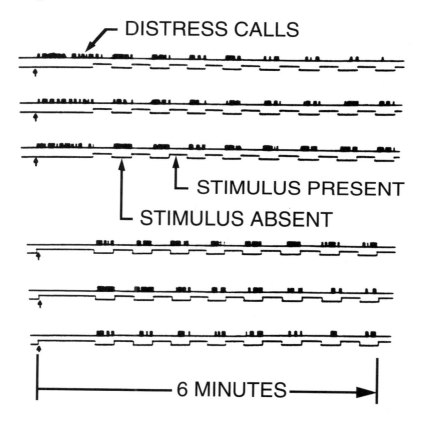

Figure 8. Records from each of six ducklings during their first exposure to an imprinting stimulus and during subsequent cycles of stimulus presentation and withdrawal. Upward excursions of the pen in the top line of each record indicate distress calls. Upward excursions of the pen in the bottom line of each record indicate stimulus presentations. The arrows indicate when the hatching box was removed.

Observations of the ducklings during the two test procedures made it clear that the cessation of distress calls with the first presentation of the imprinting stimulus could not be ascribed to a fear or a freezing response. The ducklings were very attentive to the stimulus and frequently attempted to approach and/or to follow it. In answer to our question, then, it seemed clear that under the conditions of this experiment, the very first presentation of an imprinting stimulus will immediately stop ongoing distress calls (as in the upper records in Figure 8) and will prevent distress calls if they have not yet started (as in the lower records in Figure 8).

We also carried out a number of investigations that examined what seems best described as technical questions. One series of studies (Hoffman, 1968) consisted largely of procedures that were designed to examine one or another of the possible factors that might be important in the control that the imprinting stimulus seemed to exert over distress vocalization. We wondered, for example, if this control might not depend on the change in lighting that necessarily occurred when we presented and withdrew the imprinting stimulus. To examine that issue, we arranged for the stimulus compartment to be illuminated continuously, but every now and then the train would disappear behind a barrier. We found that the ducklings would begin to emit distress calls a few seconds after the stimulus disappeared and that these calls would stop as soon as the stimulus reappeared. This made it clear that the lighting changes in the stimulus compartment were not critical to the effects engendered by stimulus presentation and withdrawal. Of course, we still did not know what the critical factor might be, or even if there was just a single critical factor. Clearly, something about the signals arising from the imprinting stimulus itself was exhibiting powerful control over our subjects' behavior. Insight into what that "something" might be was not to come for several years, after we began to direct our attention to the analysis of imprinting per se. Until then, we were more inclined to use imprinting as a research tool to study social attachment than to study imprinting itself.

4

Response Contingencies in the Domain of Imprinting

The expression "response contingency" describes the relation between a given act and the occurrence of a subsequent event in the environment. An event is said to be response contingent if its occurrence depends in some way on a given act. When we were training our ducklings to peck a key, we only presented the imprinting stimulus—the white plastic milk bottle—when the bird's behavior approximated a key peck. Once pecking began, presentation of the imprinting stimulus became contingent on the occurrence of actual pecking responses. That these response contingencies were sufficient to establish and maintain key pecking made it clear that the presentation of an imprinting stimulus has a powerful reinforcing effect.

In one of our earliest studies, my students and I sought to determine what would happen if we made the presentation of the imprinting stimulus contingent on a distress call—if we required the duckling to sound a distress call before we would present the bottle on the moving train. Our thought was that such an arrangement would reinforce distress calling. If it did, we would produce ducklings with an enhanced tendency to emit distress calls (crybaby ducklings?), just as we had previously produced ducklings with an enhanced tendency to peck the key (worker ducklings?).

Our first step, before starting the critical part of the experiment, was to imprint a group of about 20 ducklings by hatching them in isolation and then exposing them, one at a time, to the moving imprinting stimulus. When each bird had received about three hours of exposure to the imprinting stimulus, we tested that bird for its tendency to emit distress calls when we withdrew the stimulus and for its tendency to terminate distress calling when we made the stimulus visible again. The subjects were then paired so as to match them as closely as possible on both of these tendencies. The result was a set of pairs in which the two members tended to exhibit the same pattern of distress calling. In subsequent tests, we always compared each duckling with the same partner (Hoffman, Schiff, et al., 1966).

We used two imprinting units so that we could test each member of a pair simultaneously but separately. The units were located in adjacent rooms that had been sound insulated; the duckling in one room could not hear the distress calls of its partner. The important distinction between the ducklings in each room was this: distress calls by the duckling in one of the rooms would automatically cause the imprinting stimulus to be presented to itself for five seconds and at the same time, to the duckling in the adjacent room. Under this arrangement, the distress calls of the duckling in the adjacent room were recorded but had no influence on the presence or absence of the imprinting stimulus. This kind of arrangement, termed "yoking," ensured that both members of each pair would receive exactly the same number of stimulus presentations in exactly the same temporal sequence, but for only one of the ducklings would presentation of the imprinting stimulus be contingent on its distress calls. For the other duckling (the yoked duckling), stimulus presentation would bear no relation to its distress calls.

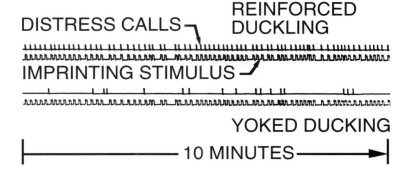

Figure 9. Sample records illustrating differences in distress calling between reinforced and yoked ducklings. In this condition, presentations of the imprinting stimulus to both ducklings were determined solely by the distress calls of the reinforced duckling.

Figure 9 shows the records from one of the yoked pairs in this study. For the reinforced duckling, the frequency of distress calls was relatively high. Its yoked partner, on the other hand, emitted relatively few distress calls. What is interesting here is that this rather sizable difference in behavior occurred despite the fact that both birds saw the imprinting stimulus at exactly the same times. Notice that the sequence of stimulus presentations in Figure 9 is identical for the two birds.The members of a pair were treated differently only in that the distress calls of one bird were producing the imprinting stimulus for both of them.

Because the two members of each yoked pair of birds showed the same differences in their rate of distress calls, it seemed clear that our original expectation had been correct. When the presentation of an imprinting stimulus is contingent on distress calls, a bird's tendency to emit these calls is strengthened. The imprinting stimulus is a powerful reinforcer.

This finding, I believe, has important implications for raising children. Consider what these data suggest would happen if, as with the reinforced duckling, a parent were to respond to a child's every whimper. The most likely outcome would be a child who did an awful lot of crying. I must admit that as a father of several young children at the time, I viewed this possibility as something to be carefully avoided. How then, should one respond to a crying child? Based on these data, it would seem that an effective way to minimize children's tendencies to cry would be to attend frequently to their needs but to do so independently of their cries.

A clue as to why this strategy should be effective is found in some of the records shown earlier. Figures 6 and 8 show that presentation of the imprinting stimulus usually caused an immediate cessation of distress calls, but that after withdrawal of the imprinting stimulus, five or more seconds usually elapsed before the birds resumed their distress calls. This lag, we suspected, could have been the critical factor in determining why the yoked ducklings emitted so few distress calls. Their reinforced partners were so prone to emit distress calls that the stimulus was seldom withdrawn for as long as 5 to 10 seconds. As a result, the yoked birds seldom had sufficient time to work themselves up to the emotional state that usually sets the occasion for distress calling.

Emotional versus Manipulative Distress Calls

An implication of this line of reasoning is that the distress calls of the reinforced birds may have been produced without emotion. Another way to put this is to suggest that the reinforced birds may have just been going through the motions of crying without experiencing the feelings that ordinarily accompany such behavior. This possibility is consistent with the observation that when ducklings have been trained to produce the imprinting stimulus by means of a key peck, they rarely emit any distress calls at all, even though the intervals between pecks, (and hence between presentations of the imprinting stimulus) are sometimes several minutes long.

In comparing the distress calls of the reinforced birds with those of their yoked partners, we could detect no differences either acoustically or through our specialized electronic equipment. The response topography gave no basis for the distinction we were making. Even without indicating differences in response topography, however, Hart et al. (1964) made a similar division of children's crying. Using a classification that B. F. Skinner (1938) had offered, they assigned crying to two classes, respondent and operant—respondent crying being the result of some painful or aversive situation, and operant crying being a means of getting attention. Hart et al. suggested that through consistent reinforcement, "crying that is initially respondent may readily become operant." It seemed to us that our results reflected a similar effect, with the imprinting stimulus replacing the mother as a reinforcer for crying.

Two additional observations were consistent with this speculation. First, although ducklings rarely sound distress calls when they have constant access to an imprinting stimulus via a key peck, it is easy to reinstate distress calling at any time. All that one needs to do is to arrange for key pecks suddenly to fail to produce the imprinting stimulus. Technically, we call discontinuing reinforcement an extinction procedure. Figure 10 shows typical patterns of key pecks, stimulus presentations, and distress calls when extinction procedures were initiated in the midst of a burst of key pecks. The records are from the same birds whose key pecks

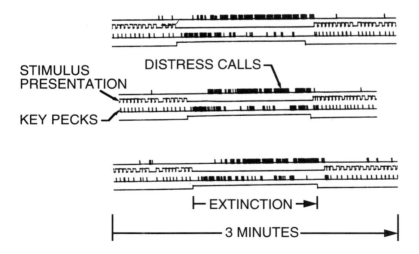

Figure 10. Key pecks and distress calls during short periods of extinction, when key pecks no longer brought about presentation of the imprinting stimulus.

had been shown in Figure 4. Now, however, in addition to showing pecks, the records depict distress calls and presentations of the imprinting stimulus. Except during the period of extinction, the birds sounded few distress calls. The onset of extinction first produced a rapid increase in the birds' rate of key pecking. This was followed somewhat later by a large increase in the rate of distress calling. With continued extinction, peck rates began to decline but distress calls continued at relatively high rates until we again allowed pecks to produce the imprinting stimulus.

A second observation that is relevant here concerns a behavioral phenomenon that occurs during the early phases of training a duckling to peck a key. Once a duckling begins to peck the key on its own, but before the response is well developed, the bird will sometimes sound distress calls for several seconds between pecks. The duckling may have already pecked a number of times but every now and then, instead of pecking the key when the stimulus is withdrawn, it emits distress calls. These usually persist until a peck finally occurs, whereupon the stimulus is again presented and distress calling ceases.

This curious behavioral pattern only occurs for a few minutes early in the training process and only the occasional duckling will exhibit it. Nevertheless, this behavior captured our full attention when we first encountered it. Indeed, we were so impressed by what it demonstrated that we devoted considerable time and energy to ensure that it would be included in a film we were making at the time (Hoffman, 1970). Our reason was quite simple. This response pattern provided the most dramatic laboratory example that any of us had ever seen of what seems best described as "self-control." In actuality, the duckling's emotional behavior (as reflected in its tendency to emit distress calls) was under the control of the presence and absence of the imprinting stimulus. But because its key pecks determined the presence and absence of the imprinting stimulus, the bird's emotional behavior was, in a sense, under its own control. Seeing this behavioral pattern and capturing it on film was a high point for me because it provided strong evidence for my growing conviction that all behavior, including such complex behavior as "self-control," is amenable to laboratory analysis if one is clever (or lucky) enough.

Imprinting and Punishment

The findings considered thus far made it clear that when the presentation of an imprinting stimulus is contingent on a particular response, stimulus presentation serves as a reinforcing event; the act that produces the stimulus begins to occur more frequently. In one phase of our early work (Hoffman, Stratton, and Newby, 1969), we asked about the corollary: what would happen if we arranged for an act not to produce the moving stimulus but to make it disappear? Would the response-contingent disappearance of the imprinting stimulus act as a punishment?

To examine this question, we used ducklings that had previously been imprinted and that had persistently followed the bottle as it moved back and forth. The idea was to try to punish this behavior by arranging that each time the duckling followed the stimulus it would break the beam of a photocell. This, in turn, would produce eight seconds of stimulus withdrawal. And so, whenever the duckling began to follow the stimulus, the stimulus would automatically disappear for a short time. If the duckling made no attempt to follow, the stimulus would remain continuously present.

The effect was clear. When following the imprinting stimulus caused it to disappear, every bird quickly ceased following. But the duckling did not ignore the stimulus. Rather, it would sit quietly for 10 to 15 minutes and simply observe the bottle as it moved back and forth. Eventually, however, the bird would again attempt to follow the bottle. If the punishment contingency had terminated, so that following could occur without the stimulus being withdrawn, the duckling did so until such time as punishment was reinstated. But if the punishment contingency was still in effect, and the attempt to follow produced stimulus withdrawal, the bird would sit down again for another 10 to 15 minutes. As we had suspected, the response-contingent withdrawal of an imprinting stimulus produced a reliable punishment effect.

It might seem to readers that this was pretty obvious. After all, what else was the duckling to do under these circumstances? The problem with that way of thinking about this and other behavioral experiments is that although the results may seem obvious in retrospect, the results we actually see are usually only one of many possible outcomes. Any of those might have seemed equally obvious. For example, if we had guessed that the ducklings would be unable to adjust their behavior of following the stimulus, would that have seemed unreasonable? If we have properly designed and performed an experiment, it will indicate which of the possible outcomes is correct and it will do so unambiguously. Our experiments were doing just that.

It is difficult to find words to convey the sense of excitement that these lines of investigation were producing for me and for my students. Throughout my own student days, first as an undergraduate at the New School for Social Research and later as a graduate student at Brooklyn College and at the University of Connecticut, I had only gradually come to the view that behavior might, in fact, be lawful, that it might be possible to understand something of its principles (or laws) if we could analyze it properly in the laboratory. Like almost everyone else I knew, I came to the study of Psychology with a strong sense that behavior has a capricious quality and that except perhaps for certain reflexes, like those studied by Pavlov, the best one can hope for is to understand something of what usually happens in a given situation. I learned how to tease out statistically significant regularity from masses of seemingly incoherent data.

What was happening here, however, was different. We were observing the kinds of systematic processes that Clark Hull (1943) and B. F. Skinner (1938) had suggested form the basis for all behavior. I had diligently studied the writings of these pioneers and had required my students also to do so. Now we were witnessing the kinds of reinforcement and punishment effects that Hull and Skinner had discussed. Moreover these effects were being demonstrated not in group averages but by individual ducklings that were only a few days old. For them, the critical event was simply the opportunity to watch and perhaps to follow a nondescript object that moved back and forth behind a transparent screen. It was as if we were being offered a glimpse of the essential nature of certain primary behavioral processes in our young subjects.

The Tale of the Acrobatic Sneezing Rat

During the time we were doing these studies, I was invited to give a talk to the local Philosophy Club. Its faculty advisor asked if I would be willing to discuss the role of reinforcement in behavior. I responded that I would happy to do so and told him that I would provide a demonstration of the power of reinforcement that I was sure his students would never forget. The talk was to be a month or so off and I was confident that with the help of my students, I would have enough time to carry off a stunt that a colleague, Thom Verhave, had mentioned to me at one of our professional meetings. In the midst of a discussion on some technical issues, he commented that for the fun of it, he had trained a rat to swing on a trapeze. I remember asking him how he had done that and he said it had been quite simple. Starting with the trapeze bar lowered to within a half inch or so of the ground, he had delivered food (reinforced a response) when the rat, in the course of its explorations, happened to touch the bar with one of its front paws. Once this behavior was occurring with some regularity, he gradually raised the bar and gradually increased the touching requirement until the animal had to leap into the air, catch the trapeze and swing back and forth a few times before food would be delivered.

When my students and I set out to train our own rat to swing on a trapeze, we found that it was easier to accomplish than I had imagined. By now, however, we were pretty skilled at presenting reinforcement contingent on a given response and we were fully aware of its immediate and powerful effects. At first, we only delivered food when the rat touched the trapeze bar with one of its front paws. On successive trials we lifted the bar a half inch or so at a time until the animal had to reach up to touch it. Once it was doing this routinely, we required it to touch the bar with both paws simultaneously and to hold them there for a brief period before we delivered food. We then raised the bar a bit more so that the rat had to stand on tip toe to meet the criterion for reinforcement. We then gradually raised the bar a fraction of an inch at a time until the rat had to jump a bit and hold on if it was to obtain food. By this time, the rat was occasionally swinging on the bar, but only in a rather perfunctory way. Our final step was to increase the response requirement and to bring the response under stimulus control. To be reinforced, the rat now had to wait for a lamp in its chamber to be illuminated and then leap almost a foot into the air, catch the trapeze with its front paws, and swing back and forth at least two times.

The lamp had been illuminated throughout training and it was only at the last stage, when the rat was swinging with ease, that we turned the lamp off for the first time. We then withheld reinforcement if the rat swung on the trapeze when the light was out, but we continued to provide a bit of food whenever it swung in the light. The end result was a rat that would leap for the trapeze when the light was turned on. Otherwise, it spent a good bit of its time watching a darkened lamp as if it was waiting for a signal to go into its trapeze swinging routine. This, I am sure, is how it looked to the members of the Philosophy club when I put on the demonstration. I announced that on cue (when I turned on a lamp in its chamber), the rat would leap into the air, grab the trapeze, and swing back and forth several times. Then I turned on the lamp and sure enough, to the delight and mystification of the audience, the rat proceeded to perform its well-learned routine. After several more demonstrations, I proceeded to indicate what I thought this implied about the nature of reinforcement and about its role in the control of behavior. I first explained how we had developed this performance by carefully arranging to systematically reinforce closer and closer approximations to the final behavior we were seeking. I pointed out that the fact that this procedure worked implied that the behavioral effects of a single appropriate reinforcement must be immediate and automatic and that they must also be reasonably large. Otherwise, the rat would not have repeated its acts and we would have found it impossible to shape the complicated set of actions that the performance required.

I also called my audience's attention to a curious aspect of our rat's performance. I had previously noticed that just before it would leap into the air to catch the trapeze, the rat would give a little sneeze. You might not notice it if you were not watching for it, but once it had been pointed out, the sneeze was quite obvious. By way of explanation, I suggested that the animal had probably sneezed at some point during the initial stages of the shaping procedure. I noted that if reinforcement had closely followed this behavior, the animal's tendency to sneeze would have been enhanced along with its tendency to engage in whatever other behavior we were deliberately reinforcing at the time. If the rat happened to sneeze again just before reinforcement, the sneeze could have become an intrinsic aspect of the behavior that was eventually established. I compared the rat's behavior to the set of special gestures that a pitcher at a baseball game will often exhibit just before the wind-up and throw. He might touch his cap or his forehead or wipe his fingers across his chest. It is a meaningless gesture, but it happens every time the ball is pitched. I pointed out to my audience that behavior of this sort is described as being superstitious. Superstitious behavior, I suggested, arises because the effects of reinforcement are immediate, automatic, and powerful. In the case of the baseball player, a casual gesture may have been followed by an especially effective pitch. If the reinforcement provided by this event was sufficiently powerful, the gesture might have been repeated, eventually becoming an intrinsic aspect of the act of throwing the ball. In the case of the rat, an accidental sneeze had, through the effects of reinforcement, become a part of the act of swinging on a trapeze.

I mention this little episode because it indicates how our thoughts about behavior were being shaped by what we were seeing in our laboratory. As I suggested earlier, I had already come to the conclusion that behavior was indeed lawful and that through laboratory studies, it would be possible to know something of those laws. This episode with the sneezing acrobatic rat served to strengthen that conviction.

5

A Conference in England

In 1970, I left The Pennsylvania State University and joined the faculty of the Department of Psychology at Bryn Mawr College. The next year, I was invited to contribute to an international conference on imprinting that was to be held at the University of Durham in England. I had been to England a few years earlier to participate in a conference on learning and had taken that occasion to visit Wladyslaw Sluckin at the University of Leicester. I had wanted to meet Sluckin ever since reading his book on imprinting (Sluckin, 1965). It had discussed this phenomenon in what I thought was an especially informative way. Before my trip, I had written and asked him if it would be possible to visit his laboratory. To my immense pleasure, he invited me to do so.

On my arrival, Sluckin and his wife, Alice, welcomed me and I spent a night or two as a guest in their home near the University's campus. Alice Sluckin is a social worker and, like her husband, knew a great deal about the phenomenon of social bonding. I remember with pleasure how the three of us spent a lively time discussing imprinting and all manner of related topics. I also remember learning that Sluckin and his wife had come to England from Poland during World War II and that they, like me, had a strong antipathy to the Nazi mentality. I had survived a year of combat as a mortar crewman in Europe during World War II and like the Sluckins, knew first hand the destructive effects this ideology had visited on the world. I mention this because it was a basis for the enduring friendship that was to develop between our two families. Years later, the Sluckins and some of their children stayed at our home near Bryn Mawr College and a few years after that, I along with my entire family descended on the Sluckins for a brief visit during a vacation trip to England.

The 1971 conference on imprinting at the University of Durham provided another opportunity for us to renew our friendship. It also gave me the opportunity to meet Konrad Lorenz, as well as a number of biologists, ethologists, and psychologists from throughout the world. They, too, all had an abiding interest in imprinting but each of us had taken our own approach to its analysis. Figure 11 shows the participants in that conference.

Standing next to me is Martin Schein, whose evening demonstration of sexual imprinting in turkeys, a number of years earlier, had sparked my interest in the area. Shortly after the turkey episode, he had moved to the University of West Virginia, and the conference provided a welcomed opportunity to spend time with an old friend.

Standing at the far right in the top row is Patrick Bateson. His research at Cambridge University, like my own, has always had a strong experimental approach and he, like the Sluckins, had stayed at my home when he visited Bryn Mawr to tell us about his latest findings.

In 1989, I participated in a second international conference on imprinting. This time, the conference was held at the University of Groningen in Holland

A Conference in England

Figure 11. A conference in England. Reading from left to right, the scientists in the top, middle, and bottom rows are: H.S. Hoffman, M.W. Schein, A.E. Salzen, F. Schultz, P.P.G. Bateson; K. Immelman, G. Gottlieb, N. Bischoff, S.J. Dimond, G.E. Macdonald, H.B. Graves, W. Sluckin; E. Fabricius, F.V. Smith, E.H. Hess, K. Lorenz, G.J. Fischer, L.J. Shapiro.

and Bateson was again one of its participants. I take note of this because one of my reasons for mentioning these two conferences is to indicate the change in the view of imprinting that occurred in the eighteen years that intervened between them.

At the first conference, the ethologists held court and Lorenz was their king. I had not previously seen anyone at a scientific conference afforded the degree of adulation that Lorenz received from some participants. One young ethologist spent most of the conference taking pictures of Lorenz. I observed him as he did so and can report that he has a picture of Lorenz eating a carrot, another of Lorenz drinking a glass of water, and if the light was right, one of Lorenz scratching himself.

53

I found it interesting to participate with Lorenz in a conference but it was also disconcerting. For all his fame (he was to be awarded a Nobel prize in 1973), Lorenz's views were idiosyncratic and in many respects, unscientific. Most disconcerting to me was his inability or unwillingness to consider the implications of the kinds of laboratory data that I and some of my colleagues were collecting. In particular, I remember his response to some data I was presenting. I do not recall the exact nature of those data, but, like all of the data I have discussed here, it consisted of recordings of some aspect of duckling behavior under carefully controlled laboratory conditions. The data were objective and I felt that they warranted objective, unbiased consideration. Lorenz dismissed those data, I suppose to the satisfaction of his followers, with the following comment: "I once knew a goose, and she was married to me, and her behavior was not like what Hoffman says." He then went into a lengthy and, I must admit, amusing discussion of his goose's behavior without ever relating it to the data I had presented. Then, because of the limited time budgeted to each of us, the discussion ended as the next participant rose to speak.

I was much disappointed by this event. I had hoped that the conference would provide a setting for a consolidation of the views of the ethologists and of psychologists like myself. This did not happen. If anything, I felt it had become more difficult for the two camps to communicate with each other.

Furthermore, it did not help matters that most of the proponents of the ethologist's position were the German members of the conference, whereas the major proponents of the psychologist's position were the American and British participants.

Although I tried to overcome my prejudices, I nonetheless viewed my German colleagues with a certain amount of emotion and suspicion. I was confident that most of them had little sympathy for the Nazi position, but they were German and I simply could not dismiss my recollections of the Nazi atrocities I had witnessed during my term as a soldier. I know that this was also true, but to an even greater degree, of the Sluckins. I have noted before that the Sluckins had managed to get to England during World War II. What I did not mention is that the Sluckins were the only members of their families to escape the Nazi gas chambers, and that Lorenz during the war had supported some of the Nazi ideology. As Bateson (1990) said in his obituary of Lorenz that appeared in The American Psychologist:

> When the Nazis came to power, he had swum with the tide and in 1940 shockingly wrote an article that dogged him for the rest of his life. He detested the effects of domestication on animal species, and he thought (without any evidence) that humans were becoming victims of their own self-domestication. His wish to rid humanity of what he regarded as impurity matched only too well the appalling Nazi ideology. Having got "our best individuals to define the type-model of our people," the unfortunates who deviated markedly from such a model should be eliminated as an act of public health. After the war in which Lorenz was to discover with horror the full scale of what the Nazis were really up to, he would have preferred this publication to have been forgotten. (p. 66).

At the meetings in Durham, Sluckin, not wishing to make a scene, planned to draw his own private line with respect to his interactions with Lorenz.

Sluckin, like me, participated fully in all aspects of the conference but near the end, we were asked to gather for a group photograph (Figure 11). As we walked to the collection point, Sluckin told me that although he had no objection to appearing in a photograph with Lorenz, he was unwilling to purchase a copy for himself. As it turned out, this slight protest was invalidated in a rather grotesque way. At the closing ceremonies, those who laid on the affair noticed that Sluckin had failed to sign up to purchase a photograph. Assuming that he had simply forgotten to do so, and in a spirit of generosity, they presented one to him—gratis. I shall never forget the look of utter dismay on the face of this wonderful albeit humble scholar when he was handed his souvenir.

The 1989 conference in Holland had an altogether different tone from the one in England. By then, the contribution of learning to the imprinting phenomenon was well accepted and the discussions centered on the nature of that learning and on the neural systems that might mediate it. In short, the phenomenon of imprinting was being carried forward into the new age of the brain and behavior. This was, of course, gratifying. Equally gratifying, however, was the fact that carefully controlled laboratory investigations were no longer criticized as being irrelevant and/or uninformative.

6

Imprinting and Eating

During the late 1960s, just before I moved the imprinting laboratory to Bryn Mawr College, our research was focused on various aspects of behavioral control by the imprinting stimulus. We had already uncovered some of the powerful reinforcement and punishment effects that occur when we make either the presentation or the withdrawal of the imprinting stimulus contingent on something the subject does. Another important aspect of that control, we were to discover, concerned the effects of stimulus presentation on the eating behavior of our ducklings. As shown in Figure 5, we had observed that when a duckling was permitted to live in the apparatus with uninterrupted access to the imprinting stimulus by means of a key peck, the bird tended to peck in bursts that were separated by relatively long intervals with few or no pecks.

Although we did not record eating and drinking in that study, it seemed to us that the duckling's tendency to engage in those kinds of behavior was somehow related to its tendency to call forth the imprinting stimulus by pecking the key. This was surprising because the key was located in the middle of the bird's compartment (Figures 1 and 2) but the food and water dishes were set against the right hand wall, several feet away. Why, we wondered, would such different kinds of behavior, occurring in such widely separated locations, be related? What was the nature of the relation?

To help answer these questions, each of several newly hatched ducklings was imprinted and then trained to produce the imprinting stimulus by pecking. By now, however, we had substituted the balsa wood pole for the key and we had replaced the white plastic milk bottle with the block of cream colored foam rubber as the imprinting stimulus. Beginning on day three, a previously imprinted bird was placed in the apparatus for a series of long (approximately 20 hours) sessions during which it could produce the imprinting stimulus for a few seconds at any time by pecking the pole. Food and water were continuously available in dishes that were located at one end of the compartment, several feet away from the pole. A pair of photocell detectors mounted over the food and water dishes made it possible automatically to record instances of eating and drinking just as we were already automatically recording pole pecks and distress calls.

Figure 12 shows several records that we obtained during this work. They indicated a strong though somewhat variable relation between a bird's eating and drinking and its production of the imprinting stimulus via pecking. As we had suspected, eating and drinking tended to occur when the birds were also pecking the pole and hence making the imprinting stimulus visible. We were onto something. We had documented the fact that a duckling's tendency to eat and drink has an important social component and our procedures

Imprinting and Eating

seemed likely to enable us to learn something of its nature.

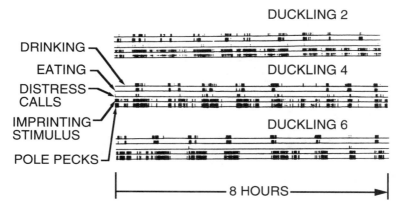

Figure 12. Eating, drinking, and distress calls during free access to food and water and to the imprinting stimulus via a pole peck.

Socially Induced Eating

Up to this point in the work, presentations of the stimulus moving across the bird's field of view had been controlled exclusively by the duckling's own behavior. In considering the response patterns in Figure 12, it seemed possible that the bird's tendency to seek out the imprinting stimulus may, at least in part, have been controlled by its feeding cycle. Some kind of reciprocal influence, however, might have existed: perhaps stimulus presentations were also influencing the bird's tendency to eat and drink. To study this last possibility, we arranged to present the moving stimulus to ducklings gratis for five minutes every hour. The birds could still view the imprinting stimulus at will by pecking the pole and they still had continuous access to food and water. Now, however, once every hour the imprinting stimulus would be presented for five minutes whether the bird pecked or not. Figure 13 shows what happened under these new circumstances.

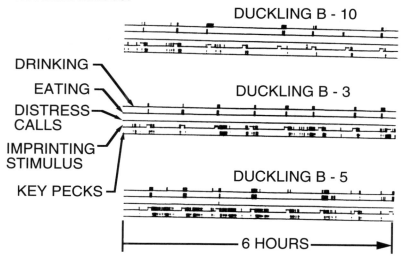

Figure 13 The effects of periodic five-minute "free" presentations of the imprinting stimulus (indicated by the wider excursions of the pen) on eating, drinking, distress calls, and pole pecks.

Once again, individual birds differed in some ways but in general, bouts of eating and drinking tended to be accompanied by and/or to follow the experimenter-initiated stimulus presentations. On many occasions, a burst of pecks also followed these bouts. As before, the birds emitted few distress calls even though the stimulus was often absent for relatively long intervals.

These data made it clear that presentation of a stimulus to which the birds had been imprinted somehow induced our ducklings to eat and drink, but at the time, we did not understand why. The phenomenon seemed related to the social facilitation of eating that Ross and Ross (1949) had studied years earlier. These investigators had induced additional eating in satiated dogs by having other dogs eat in their presence. In general, however, the various mechanisms that had been hypothesized to account for socially facilitated eating did not seem applicable to our ducklings. Explanations that required the previous pairing of eating with the social stimulus, as Harlow (1933) had suggested, proved inadequate. For example, we found that eating is induced the very first time the stimulus is presented and that this effect occurs even when ducklings have never before had an opportunity to eat in the presence of the imprinting stimulus (Hoffman, Stratton, and Newby, 1969a). Other hypotheses about socially facilitated eating, such as imitation, were also of limited value in the present context. After all, the socially facilitated eating in our experiments was induced by a block of foam rubber that merely moved back and forth behind a screen at some distance from the food. There was no eating behavior here for our ducklings to imitate.

It had seemed possible that stimulus presentations were merely serving an arousing function, but other experiments with these and other ducklings made it clear that mere arousal could not account for our findings. Figure 14 shows the results of one such experiment. It consists of a record of what happened when the imprinting stimulus was periodically presented to a duckling that previously had been able to initiate stimulus presentation by pecking the pole. Before obtaining these records, we had removed the pole from the apparatus. We see that presentation of the imprinting stimulus almost always induced some eating, with the strongest entrainment effects occurring when the interval between stimulus presentations was 20 minutes. Drinking frequently accompanied eating but it also tended to occur between eating bouts. This means that there were times when the bird was sufficiently aroused to drink and hence be near the food without necessarily eating. Stimulus presentation was doing something more than merely arousing an otherwise inactive bird.

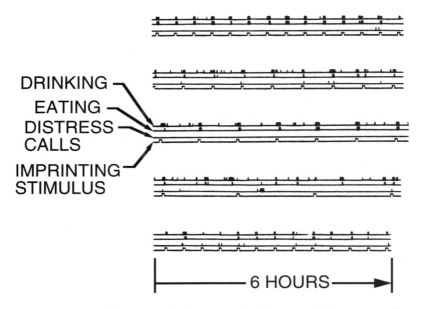

DRINKING
EATING
DISTRESS
CALLS
IMPRINTING
STIMULUS

|←——————— 6 HOURS ———————→|

Figure 14. The control of eating, drinking, and distress calls by various experimenter-initiated presentations of the imprinting stimulus to a duckling that had no other access to the imprinting stimulus.

About the time that we were doing this work, Richard Solomon at the University of Pennsylvania had begun to notice some curious behavior on the part of his pet poodle. I would only learn of this behavior many years later when Solomon and I were to collaborate on some work, but as will be seen, the actions of Solomon's dog bore a strong resemblance to those of our ducklings. This dog's behavior was to set Solomon on a course of investigation that ultimately would lead to a new theory of emotion (Solomon and Corbit, 1974). As will also be seen in Chapters 9 and 10, this theory was to have a major impact on our work and on the way we were to think about it.

For several years, Solomon had been accustomed to leaving his dog in his apartment when he left for work at 8 AM. The dog would remain there with food and water available until Solomon returned at 5 or 6 PM. This happened every day and, according to Solomon, every day the same behavior took place. With Solomon's departure, the dog would howl, wail, and moan. Eventually though, it would calm down, curl into a ball, and sleep most of the day without either eating or drinking. When Solomon finally arrived home, the dog would be overjoyed; it also would immediately rush over to its bowls to eat and drink. Solomon's dog seemed to have been exhibiting the same kind of socially facilitated eating that we had observed in our ducklings. The only major difference was that the social stimulus in our work was a moving block of foam rubber; for Solomon's dog it was Solomon himself.

I now think that the reason these social stimuli facilitate eating is that they, like eating itself, activate neural systems where pleasure is organized. I suspect that the activity of these neural systems is critical to the powerful behavioral and emotional effects that characterize the kinds of social interactions we were studying. In later chapters, after describing Solomon's theories, I will fully elaborate these ideas. For now, the important point is that we had uncovered a clear-cut interaction between social stimulation and eating, and what seemed equally important, we had learned something of its details.

7

A Critical Period For Imprinting?

In the preceding chapters, I described the care we took to ensure that our ducklings would be exposed to the imprinting stimulus moving across their field of view during the first 48 hours after they hatched. We took such care because Lorenz had observed that goslings were prone to run away from an imprinting stimulus if their initial exposure to it was postponed much beyond 48 hours. This observation prompted Lorenz to postulate a critical period for imprinting. Several laboratory experiments with ducklings, particularly those by Hess (1959a), subsequently provided strong support for this notion.

I have also described our own failures at key-peck training with birds that first encountered the imprinting stimulus when they were a week old. At the time, those failures seemed to support the notion of a critical period for imprinting. They also seemed to imply that the reinforcing properties of an imprinting stimulus derive from events that take place during the critical period. We know now that this conclusion was wrong. As will be seen, our later experiments indicated that the imprinting stimulus can reinforce behavior and suppress ongoing distress calls at the moment the duckling first encounters it. No prior exposure to the stimulus is necessary. Those experiments also indicated that, within wide limits, the point in its development when a duckling first encounters an imprinting stimulus is irrelevant. Given appropriate conditions, a duckling will become socially attached to an imprinting stimulus well after the so-called critical period.

In addition to raising questions about the viability of the notion of a critical period for imprinting, our experiments implied that the concept of a critical period in the domain of social bonding is in certain ways misleading if not altogether inappropriate. Before describing those experiments, however, it will be helpful to note how the concept of a critical period is used in the domain of developmental neurophysiology.

Critical Periods During Neurological Development

In humans and other mammals, the nervous system is incompletely developed at birth. A variety of orderly changes take place in the neuronal structure, organization, metabolism, and function of various brain systems as the architecture of the nervous system matures. Depending on the system, the functions it mediates, and its current state of development, the course of these changes is in part determined by the kinds of input the system receives. If, for example, we deprive kittens of experience with moving stimuli by rearing them under stroboscopic illumination, the proportion of direction-selective neurons in the visual cortex is greatly reduced (Cynader and Chernenko, 1976). If kittens are raised in an environment of either horizontal or vertical stripes, the proportion of cortical cells responsive to vertical stripes in the former instance and horizontal stripes in the latter is greatly reduced (Blakemore and Cooper, 1970). The time span during development in which the nervous system is susceptible to these various environmental manipulations is described as a critical period. For the cat's visual system, this period extends from approximately 2 to 14 weeks of age (Hubel and Wiesel, 1970). In humans, this period extends to about two years of age (Hickey, 1977). Adults with a history of severe early astigmatism (a condition that blurs the retinal image of lines or stripes that have a particular orientation) exhibit lower acuity for lines in that orientation even after the astigmatic error has been corrected with lenses for many years. Apparently, unless the lenses are applied during infancy when orientation-specific cortical cells are developing, the retinal input to the relevant cortical cells is inadequate, preventing the full development of those cells. This would explain why the later application of corrective lenses may correct the image on the retina but still leave an orientation-specific loss of acuity (Freeman, Mitchell, and Millodot, 1972; Mitchell et al., 1973).

The concept of a critical period for imprinting that Lorenz had articulated shared many of the features of the neurophysiologist's concept of a critical period. In both, a particular kind of sensory input must occur during a particular interval in the course of development if development is to proceed normally. If the appropriate input fails to occur during this interval, subsequent reactions to this same input are distorted.

In our own work, we had seen that when ducklings were exposed to an imprinting stimulus within a few hours of hatching—during the supposed critical period for imprinting—they followed the stimulus and emitted distress calls if it was withdrawn. If, however, we delayed this initial exposure by a few days, the ducklings reacted quite differently. Rather than approaching the stimulus, they displayed fear and attempted to flee. Both reactions, following or fleeing, were equally reliable, depending on the age at which we first exposed the duckling to the imprinting stimulus. What, we wondered, could possibly be responsible for such a dramatic change in the way that young versus older birds react when they first encounter an imprinting stimulus? In what I have always felt was one of our most informative studies, we tried to examine this behavioral change directly (Ratner and Hoffman, 1974).

Some Preparatory Work

In order to study the critical period, we first had to modify the apparatus so that we could record the ducklings' tendencies to approach or flee from the imprinting stimulus and, equally important, so that these forms of behavior would cause the stimulus to be presented or withdrawn automatically. We had previously done something like this when we arranged for stimulus withdrawal to be contingent on a following response.

Figure 15 shows the several changes we made in our apparatus. First, we inserted a vertical panel to divide the stimulus compartment in half, and we removed the lamps from the empty side. The other half of the stimulus compartment contained the imprinting stimulus. That area would be illuminated and the stimulus would move back and forth in it only when the duckling was nearby.

This was accomplished by using a set of infrared photo cells to divide the duckling's side of the apparatus into four equal quadrants. Electronic programming equipment received signals when the duckling interrupted any of the invisible photocell beams. Whenever the bird entered Quadrant 2 (immediately adjacent to the stimulus), the equipment automatically illuminated the imprinting stimulus and applied power to its train. Whenever the bird left that quadrant, the equipment automatically turned off the lamps and terminated power to the engine. With this arrangement, the stimulus was automatically presented whenever the duckling entered Quadrant 2 and remained visible and moving as long as the duckling stayed in Quadrant 2. The stimulus would, however, automatically disappear the moment the duckling moved out of this quadrant.

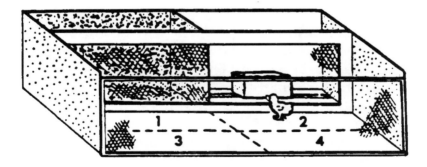

Figure 15. Apparatus used to study the critical period. The imprinting stimulus was visible only when the duckling was in Quadrant 2. If the duckling left Quadrant 2, it necessarily crossed one of the photocell beams (the dashed lines) and in doing so, caused the stimulus compartment to go dark and stimulus movement to stop. If the bird returned to Quadrant 2, the imprinting stimulus became visible again.

In preparation for the experiment that used this arrangement, a number of ducklings were hatched in isolation and thereafter were maintained in individual housing units. Twice daily, each duckling received a sequence of six 30-minute test sessions. At the start of each session, the duckling was gently lifted from its housing unit and quickly placed in the apparatus in Quadrant 2. For the next 30 minutes it was left alone and its movements into and out of the various quadrants were automatically recorded.

Several ducklings had their first test session on the day they hatched—Day 1, approximately 12 hours after the bird was free of its shell. Others had their first test session on Day 5 post-hatch. For all of these ducklings, the imprinting stimulus was visible and moving when the bird was placed in the apparatus but the stimulus would disappear for as long as the bird was out of Quadrant 2.

We also tested a number of additional ducklings. Several of these birds were first tested on Day 1 post-hatch and others on Day 5 post-hatch. The stimulus had been withdrawn before each of these birds was first placed in Quadrant 2 and, no matter where the bird might move later, the stimulus was never presented. These ducklings were intended to serve as controls for any differences in locomotor ability that might exist between one- and five-day-old birds.

We found that ducklings that never saw the imprinting stimulus (subjects in the control conditions) spent about a quarter of their time in Quadrant 2, and this tendency did not change appreciably across sessions. A more important observation for present purposes is that there were no appreciable differences in this respect between the young 12-hour-old and the more mature five-day-old control birds. In the absence of an imprinting stimulus, young and older birds displayed approximately equal locomotor activity in our apparatus. As far as these ducklings were concerned, with no imprinting stimulus available to them, all four quadrants were the same.

What about the ducklings that were exposed to the stimulus whenever they were in Quadrant 2? These birds behaved in opposite ways, depending on their age at the time of their first exposure. Birds that were 12 hours old at this time tended to stay in Quadrant 2 near the imprinting stimulus and as sessions accumulated, they spent more and more time in that quadrant. Ducklings that were five days old during their initial exposure to the imprinting stimulus fled from it immediately. Moreover, whenever they wandered back into Quadrant 2 and the stimulus again appeared, they again fled. This pattern of behavior persisted throughout the six test sessions. Because the imprinting stimulus was automatically withdrawn when a bird left Quadrant 2, these five-day-old ducklings had very little exposure to the imprinting stimulus.

The behavior of our birds provided a controlled and quantitative demonstration of the kind of observations that led Lorenz to hypothesize a critical period for imprinting. Even though afforded the opportunity to escape from an imprinting stimulus, 12-hour-old ducklings approached it. In this sense, they exhibited filial behavior. Furthermore, they continued to do so in successive sessions. When ducklings that were five days old first saw the imprinting stimulus, however, they reacted in an opposite fashion. They escaped persistently and even came to avoid the region of the apparatus where the stimulus would appear.

It is tempting to assume that these behavioral differences imply something akin to a critical period for neuronal development in the domain of social attachment. One might presume that, by being deprived of sensory input from an imprinting stimulus at a given early point in their maturation (during the period that is supposed to be critical), the neural systems responsible for social attachment fail to develop properly. This could explain why the older and younger ducklings reacted so differently in the tests performed here, and why the older birds seemed so permanently disadvantaged. Although we recognized this possibility, we also wondered if there might not be a simpler explanation, one that would not imply such ominous consequences for subsequent development.

The research literature provided us with some potentially significant leads. Several investigators had suggested that the innate developmental change that underlies what seems to be a critical period for imprinting is the age-related emergence of fear reactions to novel stimulation (Hinde, 1955; Hinde et al., 1956; Hess, 1957, 1959a,b; Candland and Campbell, 1962; Waller and Waller, 1963; Hersher, Richmond, and Moore, 1963). I shall have more to say about this proposition; much data supported it (Gray and Howard, 1957; Jaynes, 1957; Hess, 1959a; Ratner and Thompson, 1960).

Also, the critical period notion itself was called into question by a number of studies indicating that older subjects can in fact form new social alliances (Sluckin and Salzen, 1961; Bateson, 1964; Hoffman, Ratner, and Eiserer, 1972). For example, Bateson (1964) noted that although older birds at first display a strong tendency to flee from an unfamiliar moving stimulus, with continued exposure to it they gradually begin to react positively, like younger birds. Similarly, Jaynes (1958) noted that although older birds flee from a novel stimulus when exposed to it during a 30-minute session, after several such sessions they begin to approach the stimulus. Jaynes referred to this effect as "latent imprinting" and suggested that the tendency of an older bird to form a social attachment to an unfamiliar stimulus depends on the duration of the bird's exposure to the object.

Imprinting in Older Birds

In order to examine the effects of an older duckling's continued exposure to an imprinting stimulus, we kept on working with the birds we had first tested when they were five days old. We divided these birds into two groups. For one group, the conditions remained identical to those that had prevailed during the previous six sessions. That is to say, twice every day the bird was placed in Quadrant 2, with the imprinting stimulus visible and moving.If the bird left Quadrant 2, the stimulus would immediately disappear and would not reappear until the bird again entered Quadrant 2. In short, we simply continued testing these birds as we had done before; for them, nothing changed.

We treated the other birds similarly, but with a single exception. We arranged for the imprinting stimulus to remain visible and continue moving, regardless of the bird's location. Thus, although a bird in the second group might immediately leave

Quadrant 2 and then put as much distance between itself and the imprinting stimulus as possible, it could not escape completely from the sensory input the illuminated moving object provided. Under these circumstances, we expected the stimulus eventually to become familiar and hence no longer capable of eliciting novelty-induced fear.

But what would happen when this fear no longer existed? If the neural systems responsible for imprinting had in fact failed to develop properly, an older bird should be indifferent to the stimulus. Under those circumstances, it should spend about 25% of its time in Quadrant 2. If, on the other hand, competing fear responses had merely suppressed tendencies to form social attachments, then instead of reacting with indifference and spending only about 25% of its time in Quadrant 2, an older bird should begin to exhibit filial behavior: it should eventually approach and stay near the stimulus.The amount of time it spent in Quadrant 2 should increase from session to session.

The results were perfectly clear. Throughout these new sessions, birds that were permitted to escape completely from the imprinting stimulus persisted in doing so. Birds that could not completely escape did flee from Quadrant 2 at first. But as sessions accumulated and the imprinting stimulus became more and more familiar, these birds did not become indifferent to it. Instead, they spent more and more time in Quadrant 2. Eventually, by the sixth session (on Day 11 post-hatch), these older birds were spending almost all of their time near the imprinting stimulus, just like the young birds.

A Critical Period for Imprinting?

It is difficult to reconcile the behavior we had observed with the concept that the formation of a primary social bond is necessarily restricted to some brief critical period that ends a few hours after hatching. This is not to say that the notion of a critical period for imprinting is totally without merit. It accurately describes the behavior that occurs in circumstances where escape is possible, as it usually is in the natural settings where Lorenz made his observations. But the data we obtained here run counter to the assumption that the critical period for imprinting might be analogous to a critical period for neuronal development. Those data also contradict the idea that social bonding must take place during an early critical period if later problems are to be avoided. This idea was especially popular in the decades following World War II, when the "baby boom" was in full swing. During this period, much speculation focused on the likelihood of unique critical periods for all sorts of human attributes. Critical periods were proposed for the development of dependency and aggressiveness (Bloom, 1964) and for the development of linguistic skills (Scott, 1968).

In a similar vein we find the following assertions in a widely cited book (Eibl-Eibesfeldt, 1971):

> In man's development there are sensitive periods in which certain basic ethical and aesthetic attitudes become fixed as in imprinting, as for example 'primitive trust.' If such a period is allowed to pass unfulfilled, then this can lead to lasting damage. (p. 27).

Such assertions imply a conception of imprinting as an irreversible event that is limited to a brief critical period in an individual's life. They illustrate how this conception has influenced thinking about the possible long-range effects of early experience. Another example of how this conception of imprinting has influenced thinking is the theory of autism formulated by Moore and Shiek (1971). The theory states that the disorder originates when a fetus is so "neurologically advanced" that it passes through the "critical period for imprinting" before birth and as a result becomes imprinted on the womb. In support of this theory, the authors cite the notion that "once imprinting occurs, its effect cannot be reversed." This theory is rooted in the Lorenzian proposition that imprinting is an irreversible event that is limited to a brief period soon after birth.

The pronouncements stimulated by these kinds of speculations were often considered infallible and exerted a powerful influen ce on social thought. If a child was to be psychologically healthy, he or she had to experience an intimate early relationship with the mother. Any delay or interruption in this relationship, even for a short period, might result in the appearance of problem behavior later. Also, because a child who was raised in an institution was almost certain to be permanently disadvantaged, according to this view, late adoption was considered to be ill-advised. Even the placement of children in orphanages was called into question and many states abandoned their support for these institutions. As a result, many parentless or abandoned children are now left to fend for themselves. We have seen children waiting in the offices of social agencies with all of their pitifully small belongings in plastic bags while a social worker spends a late afternoon frantically trying to find these small vagabonds a single night's lodging.

In addition to its effects on conceptions of the infant's attachment to the mother, the notion of a critical period for imprinting has influenced popular views of the mother's bond to her infant. Several longitudinal studies seemed to support the proposition that unless a mother has close contact with her infant shortly after its birth, the bonding process may be slowed or even prevented. For example, Klaus and Kennell (1976, 1982) reported that in comparison to mothers exposed to normal hospital routine, mothers who were given extended postpartum contact with their infants (an hour of skin-to-skin contact within the first two hours of birth) were more attentive to their babies a month later. Other differences in behavior also seemed to differentiate the early-contact mothers from mothers not afforded this special opportunity. For example, the early-contact mothers were more likely to pick up their baby when it cried.

As Myers (1987) and Sluckin et al. (1983) noted, however, the studies that revealed these differences were fraught with methodological problems. Both Myers and Sluckin et al. also examined a wide variety of studies that failed to support the concept of a critical period for maternal bonding and both of these authors found those failures persuasive. Myers (1987) put it this way:

> Reviewing the evidence presented thus far, it is difficult to find support [for the proposition] that the postpartum period is in any way critical for human mother-infant affectional bonding. There are too many weaknesses in the "positive" studies and too many negative findings in other studies

to suggest that maternal-infant contact just after birth is...central to the mother's affection for her infant. (p. 241).

Sluckin et al. (1983) ended their thoughtful analysis of the bonding literature with the following statement:

Our message to the mother who harbors secret fears, lest she has not been properly bonded to her infant, is 'Stop worrying, your anxiety is the result of your acceptance of the bonding doctrine. It was perfectly sensible for you to believe it when no one knew better; but we now know that research findings reveal no critical period for maternal bonding, and these findings strongly indicate that maternal attachment—like child-to-adult attachment—develops in most cases slowly but surely.' (p. 97).

The results of our laboratory experiments with ducklings are in complete accord with these conclusions.

8

Imprinting and Learning

At this point in the research several features of imprinting seemed well established. First, it was apparent that a newly hatched duckling will immediately respond affirmatively when it encounters an appropriate imprinting stimulus. Second, an older (five-day-old) duckling with no history of prior imprinting will react fearfully to the same stimulus. These observations implied that some kind of fear of novelty, presumably based on a combination of maturation and experience, characterizes older birds. Third, we also knew that if an older bird is required to remain in the presence of a novel moving stimulus, it will eventually stop reacting fearfully and will begin to exhibit filial behavior. And fourth, we, like other investigators, had also observed that once a duckling has been exposed to an imprinting stimulus during the first few hours after hatching, it will react affirmatively if it is again exposed to that stimulus after several days away from it.

When we considered these observations in combination, it seemed likely that imprinting must involve the process by which the bird becomes familiar with, and in this sense learns to recognize, the imprinting stimulus. This would explain why an older, previously imprinted bird reacts affirmatively when it again encounters its imprinting stimulus. Presumably, when a young bird is exposed to an imprinting stimulus before fear of novelty (neophobia) has developed, it learns the features of the imprinting stimulus. Such learning would ensure that during later encounters with the stimulus, any tendency to exhibit a filial reaction to it will not be precluded by novelty-induced fear. There was, however, one problem with this conception: we did not know what kind of learning process might be involved. This problem had puzzled other investigators as well (Rajecki, 1973).

Our first breakthrough came when we began to consider an earlier observation that I have not yet talked about: if the foam rubber block that was to serve as an imprinting stimulus was stationary during its initial presentation to a 17-hour-old duckling, the block did not come to suppress ongoing distress vocalizations. As we pondered this observation, we soon realized its implication: to a newly hatched duckling the static features of our imprinting stimulus were at first neutral, in the sense that they did not innately evoke a filial response. If the color, shape, size, and other static features of our foam rubber imprinting stimulus were neutral, that would leave its movements as the critical imprinting factor. If so, movement of the stimulus could, through a kind of classical conditioning process, enable its originally neutral features themselves to acquire the capacity to evoke filial reactions—much like the sound of a bell came to evoke salivation when Pavlov paired the sound with the delivery of food. We reasoned that a classical conditioning process of this sort might be expected to operate if (1) visual movement of the imprinting stimulus functions as a Pavlovian unconditioned stimulus for ducklings, (2) the static features of the stimulus are initially neutral but are capable of becoming conditioned stimuli, and (3) the static features are, in effect, paired with visual movement when the imprinting stimulus is presented in motion.

A Learning Experiment

In an experiment designed to examine the role of learning in the imprinting process, previously isolated 17-hour-old ducklings were individually given an extended session in which an imprinting stimulus—the foam rubber block—was repeatedly presented and withdrawn in cycles of one minute present and one minute absent (Hoffman, Eiserer, and Singer, 1972). For subjects in the experimental condition, the imprinting stimulus was stationary during the first stimulus presentation, moved during the next, was stationary during the third, and so on. For subjects in the control condition, the imprinting stimulus was always stationary.

We found that for the subjects in the experimental condition, the block in motion always suppressed distress calling, even during its first presentation. During the alternate stimulus presentations, when the block was stationary, distress calling continued unabated at first, but as trials accumulated and the duckling had increasing amounts of exposure to the moving stimulus, the stationary stimulus came to suppress distress calls more and more completely. By the end of the experiment, its capacity to suppress distress calls was almost equal to that of the moving stimulus. Presentation of the stationary stimulus for the control subjects, who never saw it move, was totally without effect. These subjects emitted a continuous stream of distress calls throughout the session. We had to conclude that mere exposure to the stationary stimulus alone does not cause it to suppress the birds' distress calls. Before the static features of the stimulus could become effective, they had to be associated with its movement.

We conducted a similar study to determine if, through their association with visual motion, auditory features of our imprinting stimulus would also gradually acquire the capacity to suppress distress calls (Eiserer and Hoffman, 1974). A new group of previously isolated newly hatched ducklings were individually given an extended session in which an imprinting stimulus—again, the foam rubber block—was repeatedly presented and withdrawn in cycles of one minute present and one minute absent. For subjects in the experimental condition, the moving stimulus could be heard but not seen during the first stimulus presentation; it could be both seen and heard during the next; it could only be heard during the third; and so on. This was accomplished by failing to illuminate the stimulus compartment during alternate presentations of the moving stimulus. For subjects in the control condition, the stimulus compartment was never illuminated during stimulus presentation. As a result, the control ducklings repeatedly heard a moving stimulus but never saw it.

We found that for the subjects in the experimental condition, the visible block in motion almost completely suppressed distress calling, even during its first presentation. During alternate stimulus presentations, however, when the moving block could be heard but not seen, distress calling continued unabated during the first few presentations. As trials accumulated, however, and the duckling had increasing amounts of exposure to the visible moving stimulus, the sound of the stimulus in its darkened compartment came to suppress distress calls more and more. Eventually, by the end of the experiment, the sound of the moving stimulus alone was able to suppress distress calls almost to the same extent as did the visible moving stimulus. For the control subjects, who had repeated exposure to the sound but could not see the moving stimulus, the sound of the stimulus was totally without effect. These subjects emitted a continuous stream of distress calls throughout the session. We had to conclude that mere exposure to the sound of the moving stimulus alone does not cause it to suppress the birds' distress calls. Before the sound of the moving stimulus could become effective, it had to be associated with the sight of the stimulus in motion.

From these experiments, it does not take a large step to conclude that the same kind of classical conditioning occurs when a newly hatched duckling becomes attached to its biological parent in its natural environment. Like our imprinting object, the mother moves and thus provides at least one form of stimulation that innately evokes filial behavior. It is also possible that some of the static features of a mother duck, such as her shape or coloration, possess such innate capacities (Hess, 1973; Ramsay and Hess, 1954). Certain of her calls may also innately evoke filial reactions (Gottlieb, 1965). Such redundancy would function to make it all the more certain that the duckling will stay near and become socially bonded to the mother. As in our experiments, however, it is likely that other static features of the mother duck start out neutral but come to evoke conditioned filial reactions as a result of their temporal and spatial relation to the features that innately evoke the filial response.

In retrospect, it was fortunate that none of the static features of our imprinting object were innate elicitors of filial behavior. Had some static feature(s) of our object—for example, its shape or color—possessed a strong innate capacity to control filial reactions (as might have been the case if we had used a duck decoy instead of the block of foam rubber), then even the stationary object might have suppressed the distress calling of a newly hatched duckling that had never seen it in motion. Had this happened, we might never have identified the learning process that seems to be the mechanism for the formation of specific filial bonds.

Certain parallels between the behavior of our ducklings and of primates during the formation of social bonds are informative. Just as a day-old duckling will immediately exhibit a filial reaction to a moving stimulus, immature monkeys exhibit immediate filial reactions toward objects with certain tactile properties like soft, primate-size objects to which they can cling. For monkeys, as for ducklings, certain classes of stimulation innately elicit filial behavior (Harlow, 1961).

Furthermore, the learning processes elaborated in our experiments have a striking parallel in primate attachment. A stationary object did not alleviate our duckling's distress reactions until the duckling had viewed the object in motion (Hoffman, Eiserer, and Singer, 1972). Similarly, the sight of a soft surrogate object encased in a clear plastic box did not alleviate a monkey's distress reactions until the box had been removed and the monkey was permitted for several weeks to climb on and clasp the soft surrogate. Only then did the sight of the surrogate in the box come to alleviate distress (Mason, Hill, and Thompson, 1971).

Once we view imprinting as an example of learning, numerous questions come to mind. Among the most interesting is whether a duckling can be imprinted to more than one object. According to traditional conceptions, the imprinting bond that is established during the first few days of a duckling's life prevents the duckling from subsequently forming new attachments (Lorenz, 1935). If, however, imprinting is merely the process by which the young organism learns the features of stimuli that innately evoke filial behavior, imprinting to one stimulus ought not necessarily prevent imprinting to another. Indeed, under some circumstances, imprinting to one stimulus might even facilitate the development of a subsequent social bond to a different stimulus.

Imprinting to a Second Stimulus

This idea was so intriguing and ran so counter to the view of imprinting promulgated by Lorenz that we decided to examine it empirically. The first step was to find a second quite different imprinting stimulus. A series of exploratory studies indicated that a rotating amber-colored lamp, of the type used on many police vehicles, would be an effective imprinting stimulus for our birds. One experiment in which we used this new stimulus involved several conditions (Hoffman, Ratner, and Eiserer,

1972). Ducklings in Condition 1 were individually imprinted to either the moving block of foam rubber or the rotating amber lamp by giving them lengthy exposure to it during their first three days after hatching. Ducklings in Condition 2 were not exposed to either stimulus during this period. Ducklings in Condition 3 were individually exposed to both stimuli simultaneously during Days 1 to 3. We next tested each duckling on Day 5 by repeatedly presenting and withdrawing one and then the other of the two stimuli in a single session.

For ducklings in Condition 1, the stimulus to which they had been exposed on Days 1 to 3 suppressed distress calls during the test, but the calls continued unabated in the presence of the other stimulus. Ducklings that saw neither stimulus during Days 1 to 3 emitted distress calls throughout their exposure to both stimuli when tested on Day 5. For ducklings exposed to both stimuli during Days 1 to 3, only one of the stimuli suppressed distress calls—three of the five subjects in this condition had apparently imprinted to the rotating light, and the other two to the moving object. These findings made it quite clear that by Day 5 (when strong fear of novelty would have developed), ducklings that had been exposed only to one of the stimuli (Condition 1) did not react affirmatively to the other; ducklings that had been exposed to neither stimulus (Condition 2) would react affirmatively to neither; and ducklings that had been exposed to both stimuli (Condition 3) would react affirmatively to only one of them.

At this point it looked to us as though the birds would not imprint to more than one stimulus, but we carried the experiment a step further, On Day 6, each bird was given two hours of exposure to one of the stimuli in a single extended session: ducklings that on Days 1 to 3 had been exposed to only one stimulus were now exposed to the other; ducklings that had been exposed to both stimuli during Days 1 to 3 were now required to remain in the presence of the less effective (presumably nonimprinted) of the two stimuli; and ducklings that had been exposed to neither stimulus on Days 1 to 3 were exposed to one or the other (half of the group were exposed to one stimulus and the rest were exposed to the other). Within a few seconds of the start of this session and every 20 minutes thereafter, the stimulus was withdrawn for a few seconds to determine if its withdrawal would initiate distress calls and if its return would suppress them.

At first, the new stimulus seemed neutral; it exhibited very little control over the distress calls of any bird. As exposure proceeded, however, the distress vocalization of all the ducklings did come under strong control by the new stimulus. The birds came to vocalize when the new stimulus disappeared, and to stop vocalizing when it reappeared. Most interesting was the observation that the control by the new stimulus developed at different rates for birds in the three original conditions. The first birds to react to the new stimulus were those for which the stimulus had been nonpreferred during their original imprinting session; these were the Condition-3 birds that had been exposed to two stimuli during those sessions. Ducklings that had been imprinted to a different stimulus (Condition 1) also came under the strong control of the new stimulus by the end of the session. Ducklings with no prior imprinting experience at all (Condition 2) did not come under very strong control during the 120-minute exposure period. Two hours of additional exposure, however, brought their distress calls under the strong control of the stimulus, approximately to the same extent as the other birds.

This configuration of results demonstrated to us that imprinting to one stimulus neither prevented nor retarded imprinting to a second stimulus. Instead, it facilitated the development of control by a second stimulus. Ducklings that had previously been imprinted to one stimulus imprinted more rapidly to a new stimulus than did ducklings that had not previously been imprinted.

We repeated variations of this experiment over the years and found that if conditions are appropriate, ducklings will readily change the object of their filial bond. We also found that in addition to its control over distress vocalization, a second distinctive imprinting stimulus can elicit following and can reinforce other behavior (for example, pecking a pole) just as the original imprinting stimulus does. Furthermore, an experiment by Mason and Kenney (1974) with monkeys revealed a similar pattern. Rhesus monkeys were raised with their own natural mothers or with a claspable mother surrogate until they were three to ten months old. They were then removed from these sources of social stimulation and were exposed to friendly female dogs. At first, the monkeys showed all the signs of fearfulness, but by the end of one day they approached the dogs, clung to them, and were soon following them. They, too, had formed a new social bond.

9

The Motivational Substrate for Imprinting

I n view of the immediacy of a duckling's filial reaction to an imprinting object, one might suppose that this reaction reflects an intrinsic need for the kind of stimulation the object provides. Indeed, Bateson (1971) has reported that before a newly hatched duckling ever sees an imprinting object, it often emits what seems to be "appetitive behavior" that terminates only when the bird sees the object. Because this behavior includes distress calls, it might be taken to reflect an intrinsic need that is aversive. There is, however, a problem with this inference. One cannot know if the ducklings' distress calls before they have seen an imprinting stimulus reflect an intrinsic need for that stimulus, or if the calls are a reaction to an environment that is itself aversive and therefore would by itself induce distress. What would happen, we wondered, if we were to expose ducklings to an imprinting object in a setting that was completely comfortable and hence would not itself induce distress calling?

Is There an "Intrinsic Need" for an Imprinting Stimulus?

In an experiment designed to examine this issue (Hoffman and Ratner, 1973a), we monitored the incubating eggs and when an egg first revealed pip marks, we transferred it to the apparatus and permitted the duckling to hatch in the illuminated subject compartment, with the imprinting stimulus withdrawn and hence not visible. We permitted the bird to remain in this environment, isolated and undisturbed, for 17 hours. By using a portable heater and humidifier, we kept the temperature and humidity the same as in the incubator. Our intention was to make the bird as comfortable as possible.

We observed the duckling's behavior throughout this period by means of a TV camera and a remote monitor. Each duckling that we tested explored its environment and sometimes rested, but none gave any sign of missing an imprinting stimulus. Moreover, although a few birds sounded an occasional single distress note, most birds sounded none. At the end of the 17 hours, we suddenly illuminated the stimulus compartment and powered the engine that carried the block of foam rubber; the moving imprinting stimulus was presented for the first time. When the stimulus had been present for 10 minutes, we extinguished the lights in its compartment and terminated the power to its engine, thereby returning the duckling to the stimulus conditions that had been in effect just before stimulus presentation.

No distress calls occurred at any time during the 10 minute presentation of the imprinting stimulus, but all the ducklings appeared to be interested in it; some merely looked in its direction but others followed it as it moved along its tracks. In contrast, the behavior of the ducklings when we finally withdrew the stimulus (after 10 minutes) was uniform. Every bird began to emit distress calls that persisted for several minutes. These calls were especially interesting because they occurred in an environment that was identical to the environment as it had been 10 minutes previously, just before we presented the imprinting stimulus.

Our ducklings, then, displayed no evidence of an inborn need for an imprinting stimulus. If such a need existed, one would have expected it to become somehow apparent during the 17 hours that preceded stimulus presentation. This did not happen. Before their exposure to the imprinting stimulus, the ducklings were quite calm and emitted few distress calls. Of course, it was possible that a need state might have become apparent if the ducklings had been deprived of the imprinting stimulus for more than 17 hours. Whether it would or not, our findings made it clear that mere exposure to an imprinting stimulus was itself sufficient to generate a rather powerful need for further contact with it.

Some Efforts at Theory Construction

While we were puzzling over the implications of this finding, a series of events occurred that were to clarify the whole issue. They began when I was invited to present a talk about our imprinting research to the Psychology Department at the University of Pennsylvania. When I gave the talk, I was especially pleased to note that Professor Richard Solomon was in the audience. While I was a graduate student at the University of Connecticut, I had studied Solomon's research on avoidance behavior and had been so impressed by the kinds of insights it provided that I had consciously decided to try to emulate his approach in my own work. To have Solomon in my audience was therefore a distinct honor for me. The talk went well and generated some interesting discussions, although I do not remember that Solomon participated in them.

A week or two later, I was again asked to talk about our imprinting research but this time I was to speak to the Psychology Department at Temple University which, like Bryn Mawr and the University of Pennsylvania, is also in the Philadelphia area. I am sure readers can envision my surprise when I noticed that Professor Solomon was again seated in my audience. After the talk, when the questions had been answered and we were having refreshments, I asked him why he had come to the talk at Temple when he knew I was certain to present the same material I had covered a few weeks earlier at Penn. He replied that he had found our work to be directly relevant to a theory of motivation and emotion that he and John Corbit at Brown University were developing. He wanted to be sure that he had understood the details of our findings and he wondered if he and some of his students could visit my laboratory to discuss some possible collaborative research. I, of course, was enormously pleased by this opportunity and a few weeks later, Solomon and some of his graduate students paid us a visit.

I recall that after I showed them our laboratory, Solomon described his theory and indicated how we might be able to test some of the predictions it generated. The theory was originally designed to account for the dynamics of behavioral control by aversive stimuli and for many of the motivational processes that are observed in addictions (Solomon and Corbit, 1974). According to this theory, the onset and maintenance of an affect-arousing stimulus creates a primary motivational condition or state. Depending on the nature of the stimulus, this state can be either negative (as with a fear producing stimulus) or positive (as with our imprinting stimulus). The theory also holds that the occurrence of this state automatically arouses, via an opponent-loop system, an affective process that opposes the original state and reduces its intensity. And finally, the theory postulates that opponent processes are slow to develop and, once the original stimulus is removed, slow to dissipate. These characteristics of opponent processes lead to the interesting prediction that if a duckling's initial exposure to an imprinting stimulus takes place in a comfortable environment, and if the stimulus presentations are brief, the opponent process should develop gradually. In imprinting, the opponent process would be hedonically negative. Therefore, during the presentation of an imprinting stimulus, this opponent process should gradually get stronger. One would not necessarily see this effect with a 10-minute stimulus presentation (as in the previous study) because the opponent process might have reached a near-maximum level in 10 minutes. If, however, stimulus presentations occur frequently but only briefly each time, one should be able to observe a gradual growth in the opponent process as reflected in the ducklings increasing tendency to emit distress calls when the stimulus is withdrawn.

A Test of Opponent Process Theory

In order to test this prediction, we repeated the basic procedures we had used in the previous experiment. This time, however, rather than affording the ducklings a single 10-minute exposure to the imprinting stimulus, we presented the stimulus many times but only for one minute each time (Hoffman et al., 1974). As in the earlier study, very few distress calls occurred during the 17 hours before the initial stimulus presentation or during later stimulus presentations. Unlike the immediate and strong post-stimulus distress vocalization in the previous experiment, however, the birds' distress calling in the post-stimulus periods now developed only gradually.

Figure 16 shows this pattern of distress calling. With repeated stimulus presentations, withdrawal of the stimulus occasioned more and more distress calls in exact accord with the predictions of opponent process theory. According to this theory, the distress vocalization that ensues when an imprinting stimulus is withdrawn is a reaction to the opponent process that has developed during stimulus presentation and that lingers after stimulus withdrawal. If stimulus presentations and withdrawals are relatively short, the effects of repeated stimulus presentations should be cumulative. This would explain the difference in the post-stimulus pattern of distress calls in the previous and present experiment. In the previous experiment, stimulus presentation lasted for 10 minutes. Presumably, this was enough time for the opponent process to build to a high level; hence

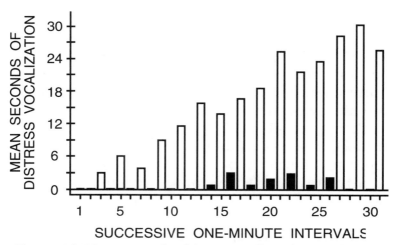

Figure 16. Mean seconds of distress calling during alternate one-minute periods of stimulus presentation (solid bars) and stimulus withdrawal (open bars). Each duckling in this study was placed in the apparatus when it was first free of its shell and remained there alone and undisturbed with the stimulus withdrawn until testing began 17 hours later.

the high level of distress calling that ensued when we finally withdrew the stimulus. In the present experiment, each stimulus presentation lasted for only one minute. Accordingly, it took a number of presentations before the opponent process could grow strong enough to produce a substantial amount of distress calling.

Considered together, the results of these two experiments have important implications for an understanding of the attachment that imprinting ultimately entails. In particular, they imply that independent of any intrinsic need, exposing a duckling to an imprinting stimulus creates its own need; within limits, the longer the exposure, the greater the need.

Some Related Pharmacological Studies

It is of special interest that data consistent with this interpretation of social bonding have been obtained from pharmacological studies. Panksepp and his associates (Herman and Panksepp, 1978; Panksepp et al., 1978) found that separation-induced distress calling by newly hatched chicks could be alleviated by intraventricular injections of minute quantities of either morphine or endorphins. In contrast, separation-induced distress vocalization could be enhanced by injections of a morphine antagonist (naloxone). Furthermore, other work in Panksepp's laboratory indicated that even in large doses, tranquilizers, barbiturates, and amphetamines were unable to alleviate separation-induced distress calling. This evidence supports the concept that the production of opiate-like peptides mediates social bonding. If one adds to this concept the idea that the stimulation provided by an imprinting stimulus initiates the production of these substances, it would explain why newly hatched ducklings immediately react affirmatively to such a stimulus.

The idea that an imprinting stimulus initiates the production of opiate-like peptides can also explain why such a stimulus can calm a frightened subject and why its withdrawal is so aversive. This idea also explains why, as was seen in Figure 16, ducklings that were otherwise comfortable began to emit distress calls in the absence of the stimulus only after they had some exposure to it.

These considerations point to the conclusion that in the domain of social bonding, much is to be gained by viewing the behavior it entails as exemplifying a kind of addiction. Furthermore, if social bonds are mediated by the production of endorphins, then one should expect to find many parallels between imprinting in ducklings and social bonding in other organisms—nonhuman and human. In the next chapter, I describe some of those parallels.

10

A Mystery Finally Solved

When given unlimited access to an imprinting stimulus via a peck to a key or pole, with each peck producing the stimulus for a few seconds, ducklings invariably peck in bursts that are separated by more or less extended intervals without pecks. As I noted in Chapter 2, when we first observed this behavioral pattern, we thought it might represent mere random fluctuations in a bird's tendency to peck. A detailed statistical analysis of the data, however, made it clear that something other than chance was at work. When we tried to determine what that "something" might be, we ran into a stone wall. At first, we were confident that some sort of deprivation and satiation effects, related to the duckling's intrinsic need for social stimulation, must be responsible. The data, however, did not support this notion. Had deprivation and satiation processes been at work, we would have found longer bursts after the stimulus had been absent for longer periods. We would also have found longer periods without pecking to follow longer bursts. Our analysis, however, failed to provide even a hint of these relations.

So there we were. Our birds were exhibiting a distinctive and highly reliable pattern of behavior and why they were doing so was a complete mystery. The mystery became all the more puzzling when I began to notice my own children exhibiting what seemed like the same sort of behavioral pattern we saw in our ducklings. My daughter, a toddler at the time, was often content to play alone, sometimes out of my sight for many minutes. Eventually, however, she would stop playing, seek me out, climb into my lap, and nestle there for several minutes. Finally, she would climb down and go back to what she had been doing or begin another activity. The pattern would then repeat itself. Her contacts with me were not just momentary. She did not play for a while and then simply check in to see if I was still there before continuing with her play. It was as if she needed a certain quota of contact each time she came to me. I also noticed the same pattern of behavior at the cooperative nursery school our children attended, where my wife and I occasionally served as teacher's assistants. For example, a child would sometimes play contentedly with blocks for several minutes. At some point, though, the child would seek out the teacher or her assistant and seem to require a certain amount of sustained attention. What I did not see was children who would periodically leave their play activity, check in briefly with an adult, and then quickly return to what they had been doing.

Over the years, I had pondered this pattern of responding in bursts. I sensed that it had to reflect a basic aspect of the way social bonds are maintained, but it was a graduate student (now Dr. Peter DePaulo) who had the insight into what might be responsible for this pattern (DePaulo and Hoffman, 1980). Peter suggested that if social attachments are mediated by the release of endorphins, bursts of responding might be an expected effect of the opponent processes that Solomon and Corbit (1974) had proposed to explain addictive behavior.

In particular, Peter suggested that recordings of bursts should exhibit two kinds of sequential dependencies. One of these, the probability that a duckling will continue a burst once it had been initiated, should increase as the total number of recent exposures to an imprinting stimulus grows larger and the opponent process grows stronger. The other, the probability that a duckling will initiate a new burst, should decrease as time since the prior burst grows longer and the opponent process wanes.

The Data

To test Peter's proposal, we trained each of a number of ducklings to peck a pole, using a brief view of the imprinting stimulus as the reinforcing event. We then gave each bird a large number of two-hour sessions in which a peck during stimulus withdrawal provided a 10-second view of the moving stimulus. (As in prior studies, pecks during stimulus presence were without effect and they rarely occurred.) Every bird displayed the usual pattern of pecking in bursts.

Having collected the data, we evaluated the two types of sequential dependencies. First, we examined the records to determine how the likelihood of continuing an ongoing burst might depend on the number (and hence the total duration) of the prior stimulus presentations in that burst. The second analysis determined how the likelihood of initiating a new burst might depend on the amount of time that had elapsed since the end of the previous burst.

Figure 17 shows the results of the first analysis. For this analysis, a group of temporally proximate stimulus presentations were defined as belonging to a single burst if no more than 30 seconds elapsed between any two stimulus presentations. Burst size was then defined as the number of stimulus presentations in a burst. For each bird, we tallied the frequencies of bursts of Size 1, Size 2, Size 3, and so on. These frequency tallies were then used to determine the probability that the bird, having produced a burst of a given size, would continue

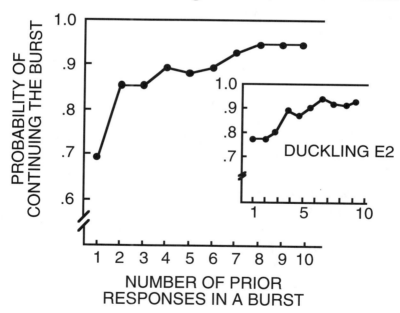

Figure 17. Probability of extending a burst as a function of the current size of the burst. (Adapted from DePaulo and Hoffman, 1980.)

the burst (by emitting another peck within the next 30 seconds).

The inset in Figure 17 shows these probabilities for Duckling E2. The larger function in Figure 17 shows the same probabilities but is based on the pooled frequencies across six birds. The first data point shows the probability that a duckling, having produced the first stimulus presentation of a given burst, would continue the burst by producing at least one more stimulus within the next 30 seconds. This probability was obtained by dividing the number of bursts of Size 2 or greater by the number of bursts of Size 1 or greater (that is to say, by the total number of bursts). The second point represents the probability that a burst that already contains two stimulus presentations would continue. It was obtained by dividing the number of bursts of Size 3 or greater by the number of bursts of Size 2 or greater. Each point, then, was obtained by dividing the number of bursts of Size N + 1 or greater by the number of bursts of Size N or greater. This computational procedure compares the number of opportunities for a burst of a given size to be continued with the number of times that a burst of that size actually was continued.

As seen in Figure 17, the longer the burst that the duckling was currently producing, the more likely it was to continue the burst. Apparently there is no constraint on the size of a burst. (A burst eventually ends, of course, because the probability of responding at each new opportunity to lengthen the burst is always less than 1.0.)

Figure 18 shows how the probability of a peck changed as a function of the time elapsed since the end of the previous burst. The functions in Figure 18 were derived from the frequency

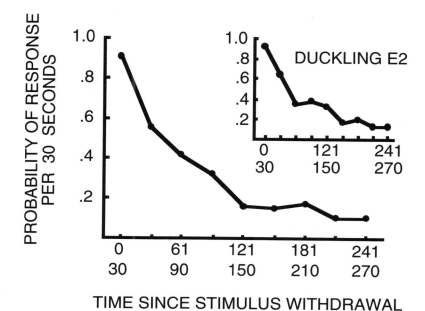

Figure 18. Probability of a peck as a function of the time since stimulus withdrawal. (Adapted from DePaulo and Hoffman, 1980.)

distribution of intervals between the withdrawal of a given stimulus and the occurrence of the next peck. Again, the function in the inset is based on Duckling E2's performance and the larger function was derived by pooling the data from six birds. The first point indicates the probability of a peck within 30 seconds of the termination of a given stimulus presentation. This probability was obtained by dividing the number of interstimulus intervals of thirty seconds or less by the total number of interstimulus intervals. Similarly, the second point represents the probability that a duckling, having failed to peck in the first 30 seconds after stimulus withdrawal, would peck within the next 30 seconds (in the interval that occurred 31 to 60 seconds after stimulus withdrawal); it was obtained by dividing the number of interstimulus intervals of 31 to 60 seconds by the number of opportunities for this interstimulus interval to occur (the total number of interstimulus intervals of 31 seconds or longer). Each point, then, indicates the number of interstimulus intervals between X and Y seconds divided by the total number of interstimulus intervals that were X seconds or longer.

Figure 17 shows that the longer a burst that a duckling was currently producing, the more likely it was that the burst would continue. Figure 18 shows that the longer a duckling went without seeing the imprinting stimulus, the less likely it was to seek it out by pecking the pole. The popular conception of attachment would not have led us to expect this result. Absence did not make the heart grow fonder and familiarity did not breed contempt. Indeed, just the opposite occurred.

When we considered the full implications of these findings, we realized that the mystery of the burst pattern of responding had been solved. The birds respond in bursts because they are reacting to changes in their affective state that, according to opponent process theory, must occur when they encounter a stimulus that elicits endorphins and that stimulus is then withdrawn. Rather than reacting to an intrinsic need, such as the need for food or water, a bird seeks out an imprinting stimulus in bursts because it is reacting to the dynamics of an addiction.

Implications for Primates and Humans

If, as implied by opponent process theory, the production of endorphins mediates the affect aroused in primates and humans during social interactions, as it is presumed to do in ducklings, then one ought to be able to find parallels between the attachment behavior of primates (including humans) and of ducklings. As it turns out, many striking parallels exist. Just as one-day-old ducklings will immediately exhibit filial reactions toward an appropriate imprinting stimulus, immature monkeys will exhibit immediate filial reactions toward soft objects to which they can cling (Harlow, 1974). For monkeys, as for ducklings, certain classes of stimulation innately elicit filial behavior. Similarly, as every parent knows, a newborn infant's response to being cuddled and stroked is immediate and unlearned. It takes no great stretch of the imagination to guess that there is a common mechanism in operation here, that for each of these species, certain classes of stimulation are able innately to elicit the production of endorphins.

One may also suppose that through a learning (conditioning) process, certain classes of initially neutral stimulation could come also to elicit the production of endorphins. For our ducklings, the static visual features of the imprinting stimulus as well as the sounds of its engine were at first unable to elicit the production of endorphins and hence to suppress distress calls. Whenever the imprinting stimulus was seen in motion, however, its static visual features as well as the sounds of its engine were also seen and heard. As a result of this association, these initially neutral features of the stimulus gradually acquired the capacity themselves to elicit the production of endorphins and thereby to suppress distress calls. Likewise, for human infants, one might suppose that certain features of the mother's face, voice, and so on, that distinguish her from other people, are initially neutral and do not evoke filial reactions until they are paired with those aspects of the mother that do innately elicit the production of endorphins with their accompanying filial responses.

These comparisons help place imprinting into evolutionary perspective. As noted by Jacob (1977):

> Evolution does not produce novelties from scratch. It works on what already exists, either transforming a system to give it new functions or combining several systems to produce a more elaborate one. (p. 1164).

It appears that imprinting is no exception to Jacob's principle. Most if not all of the seemingly distinctive features of imprinting in ducklings appear to be the product of a limited number of basic behavioral processes that are seen in a wide variety of other species. One such process is represented by the immediate filial reaction that many organisms exhibit to certain classes of stimulation. Another is represented by the capacity to profit from experience, to learn. Even insects exhibit this capacity. A third such process is maturational. It entails an increasing tendency to be fearful of novel stimulation as the duckling grows older. The fear of strangers that human infants exhibit at about eight months of age is similar to the novelty-induced fear that older ducklings exhibit.

In addition to providing a reasonably unified picture of social bonding across a variety of species, the idea that attachment behavior is based on an interaction among opposing processes can explain why this behavior sometimes exhibits wide variations across species and among individuals within a species. One need only consider the way these processes might interact in a natural setting.

At first, some aspect of an appropriate attachment object provides stimulation that innately elicits filial behavior. It does so by stimulating the production of endorphins. If the organism has had extended exposure to such an object, the initially neutral features of the object will also come to elicit filial behavior through a learning process that seems best described as classical conditioning. Once this learning has occurred, the attachment object will have been rendered familiar, able to maintain the organism's tendency to respond filially after the tendency to respond fearfully to unfamiliar stimuli emerges.

Considering the complexity of these interactions, it is no wonder that the attachment phenomenon should exhibit so many ramifications. The possibilities for variations across species and for individual differences are enormous. A given organism or species might, for example, be more or less sensitive to a given form of eliciting stimulation. There must be individual as well as cross-species differences in rates of learning and in the maturational factors that contribute to novelty-induced fear. In short, there is ample opportunity for the variations in social bonding that evolution appears to have produced.

11

Aversive Stimulation

The Use of Nonhuman Subjects

As every scientist knows, nature does not give up its secrets easily; each must be purchased at some expense and sometimes at some risk. In the behavioral sciences, as in much of medicine, every item of new information has a price and it is often an animal subject who pays it. At the least, a subject may only be inconvenienced for a brief period. At the worst it may be required to pay dearly, even forfeiting its life at the end, as in certain medical studies. Because I saw no way to circumvent this problem and because I was fully committed to the value of animal subjects, I decided at the start of my scientific career that in my own research I would try to purchase new information as cheaply as possible. For every project, I would try to determine if the information being sought was likely to be worth the price the animals would have to pay. If there was a chance, even a remote one, that human lives might be bettered or saved by the application of knowledge derived from the research, it would justify some aversive procedures. Otherwise, there would be no justification for inflicting pain.

Some of my colleagues have had their laboratories ransacked and their animals stolen by members of various animal rights groups. Moreover, government regulations, imposed as a response to the protests of these groups, have enormously increased the cost of research. Now, the care of one's animals is an important consideration not only to avoid pain and discomfort for them but also to avoid the personal insensitivity that a failure to do so would engender. But I have been alarmed and sickened by the fact that in the area where I live, the housing and care provided for experimental animals is now better than that provided for homeless children.

The issue came into focus for me when I encountered a letter to the editor entitled "The moral status of mice" (Herzog, 1988). The author pointed out that in the medical building where he did his research, millions of dollars had been spent to ensure that its animal care facilities would comply with the regulations that university and government officials were developing in response to pressure from the animal rights lobby. In his building, the result was the creation of two classes of mice: the good mice and the bad mice. The good mice were the experimental animals. These were housed in immaculate quarters, with their care and treatment closely supervised by a team of professionals whose principle duty was to ensure that the new regulations were scrupulously followed. The bad mice also resided in this building but their quarters were far from immaculate. Usually, they consisted of dark, filthy, out-of-the-way corners that were difficult if not impossible to find. Most of the time, the bad mice kept to their self-selected quarters but occasionally one of them might be seen scurrying along a hall as it foraged for food. When this happened, every effort was made to do away with the animal. No method, no matter how potentially painful, was considered inappropriate. Traps could be set, poison bait could be scattered about, or sticky paper could be laid down in the hope that the animal might entangle itself. Unlike the good mice, whose rights were being zealously guarded, the bad mice had no rights at all. This, Herzog noted, was a curious state of affairs; most of the bad mice had formerly been good mice that had escaped from their luxurious quarters.

This story does not argue that the use of animals in research should be unsupervised but it points to the futility of trying to achieve ethical treatment of laboratory animals by regulation only. Ethics on the part of investigators (and regulators) is also required. Fortunately, with only a few exceptions, the investigators I have known over the years have struck me as being highly ethical men and women.

I had considered the issue of the ethical treatment of animals and my own feelings about it at the beginning of my research career. It would have to be reconsidered many more times as that career unfolded, and it was reconsidered in the context of imprinting when I and my students were trying to decide whether we should undertake to investigate how brief electric shocks might influence our ducklings' filial reactions. After some debate, we decided to proceed with the investigation because we felt it might produce information that could lead to a better understanding of the effects of aversive procedures during the bonding process in children. We recognized that some would say that research on ducklings can have no relevance to humans but, as I have indicated throughout this book, this was never our position.

The Basic Technique

Once we decided to use aversive stimulation, we had to find a way to do so safely and effectively. Because we would need control over exactly how and when the stimulation was to be delivered, we decided to work with mild electric shock. A length of finely-linked gold chain was wrapped around the base of each of a bird's wings. The gold chains were connected to flexible hairlike wires that hung from a swivel system that was mounted above the subject's compartment (Barrett, Hoffman, Stratton, and Newby, 1971). This arrangement allowed the subject freedom of movement throughout its compartment while making it possible for us to deliver the electric shock as needed. A beam of infrared light was focused across the subject's compartment so that if the duckling followed the stimulus, it would break the beam. This allowed us to record the duckling's following behavior automatically and to deliver shock automatically, contingent on the occurrence of this activity.

Some Findings and Their Implications

Kovach and Hess (1963) had reported that when brief electric shocks were occasionally delivered while ducklings were being imprinted, their tendency to exhibit filial behavior was enhanced; they followed the imprinting stimulus more closely. Also, Moltz, Rosenblum, and Halikas (1959) had found that the tendency of newly hatched ducklings to follow an imprinting stimulus was also enhanced when shock was delivered before rather than during the imprinting session. We later confirmed this finding in our own laboratory when Alan Ratner found enhanced following even though shock was only delivered during periods when the imprinting stimulus had been briefly withdrawn (Ratner, 1976).

In these studies, shock delivery was never explicitly contingent on either a specific response or the presence of the imprinting stimulus. Considered together, they imply that with imprinting, the delivery of shock can have motivational effects that enhance a duckling's tendency to follow and stay near an imprinting stimulus. They also imply that these motivational effects are independent of a direct association between the shock and either the imprinting stimulus or a given response.

We therefore set out to learn what happens when shock is made contingent on a specific response. It turned out that a subject's tendency to make that response is reduced, even if it is a filial reaction that is usually directed toward an imprinting stimulus. When James Barrett arranged for brief shock to be contingent on the occurrence of a duckling's following response—explicitly punishing the bird for following—his ducklings eventually stopped following the stimulus until the contingency ceased to be in effect (Barrett, 1972). In this respect, the ducklings behaved in the same fashion as when we had arranged the response contingencies so that following led to stimulus withdrawal (Chapter 4).

All of this means that in the context of imprinting, aversive stimulation has complex effects. The mere occurrence of an aversive stimulus can enhance the motivational substrate that supports filial behavior. But if the delivery of the aversive stimulus is restricted to occurrences of a given response, that response can be suppressed—even though the response (for example, following) might be an aspect of the filial behavior that would otherwise be enhanced.

Finally, we found that aversive stimulation can influence the behavior that characterizes imprinting in another rather interesting way. As noted above, when newly hatched ducklings receive response-independent shock in the presence of an imprinting stimulus, they tend to follow it more closely than do birds that never receive shock. This, of course, is consistent with the conclusion that aversive stimulation enhances the motivational background for the expression of filial behavior. Both Barrett (1972) and Ratner (1976) also found, however, that when they discontinued the use of shock and offered the ducklings a choice between their original imprinting stimulus (the foam rubber block) as it moved back and forth at one end of the stimulus compartment and a novel moving stimulus simultaneously presented at the other end of the compartment, their choice depended on the resemblance between the new and the original stimuli. If the new stimulus was sufficiently novel (when, for example, it was a rotating lamp), the birds approached and stayed near their original imprinting stimulus. When, however, the new stimulus was another block of foam rubber that had been rendered perceptually distinctive (by painting black stripes on it), they approached and followed the new stimulus and eschewed their original imprinting stimulus. Because these studies included controls for any inherent differences in preference that the two stimuli may have afforded, and because Ratner's study revealed that the effect is not obtained when shock delivery is restricted to periods of stimulus withdrawal, it is apparent that ducklings, like most other organisms, can also associate aversive events with the stimulation that prevails at the time. If that stimulation includes an object that elicits filial behavior (for example, an imprinting stimulus), the bird's tendency to approach and stay near the object is enhanced. If, however, the duckling is subsequently permitted to choose between approaching its original imprinting stimulus and an alternative imprinting stimulus that is not too novel, it will choose the alternative stimulus.

It turns out, then, that many of the effects engendered by aversive stimulation with ducklings in the context of imprinting are basically the same as are obtained with other organisms in more traditional contexts. In those contexts, aversive stimulation has been found to have a motivational or arousing effect, as well as a variety of associative or learning effects. Ducklings exhibit the same kinds of effects in the context of imprinting. What seems equally important is that they exhibit these effects in ways that may help us understand what happens when aversive stimulation is delivered in the course of human social bonding.

Certainly, what happens when a human parent is physically abusive is not precisely the same as what happens when ducklings receive electric shocks in the presence of an imprinting stimulus. With humans, the results of abuse are likely to be more complex because people are more complex than ducklings. But if society is to understand what happens to social bonding when a child is physically abused, and if it is to learn how best to correct or prevent those effects, it will have to start somewhere else then by doing experiments with people. I think we have made a reasonable start by taking a hard look at what happened when we used aversive stimulation in the context of imprinting. Our results justify at least the suggestion that a physically abused child may become more closely attached to an abusive parent. This is essentially what our ducklings did when they received electric shocks in the presence of a stimulus on which they had been imprinted.

Our results also give some hope that if an abused child must be placed with a substitute parent, the child itself might aid in the transition. When our ducklings were given a choice between an imprinting stimulus that had been present when they received shocks and a new stimulus that was not too different, the birds spontaneously shifted their affiliation to the new stimulus. The heightened attachment that abuse may generate is, therefore, transferable. In view of nature's continuity, it seems quite possible that a similar effect may obtain with humans.

12

Aggression and Imprinting

When we permit several ducklings to live together by housing them in the same unit, we rarely observe any behavior that even remotely resembles aggression. If, however, we remove one of the birds from the group, housing it in isolation for several days, it behaves aggressively when we subsequently return it to the group. Every now and then, it approaches one or another of the birds and directs an intense peck at its head or back.

I recognize that to describe this behavior as aggressive implies that the duckling making the peck was motivated to inflict injury. Although there was no way to ask the bird if this interpretation was in fact correct, observations of the target birds' reactions made it clear that those birds found the pecks highly aversive. Besides immediately trying to withdraw, the target birds frequently responded with distress calls. Some even tried to jump out of the housing unit. This did not surprise us because the pecks were, at times, strong enough to knock the target bird onto its side or back and even to draw blood. Sometimes a target bird was seen to peck back, but this was rare. The most common reaction to being pecked was an attempt to flee and the most common response of the attacker was to follow the target bird and peck at it again.

This type of aggressive behavior, called isolation-induced aggression, has been observed in a wide variety of species: chicks, mice, rats, and primates. It is a characteristic of these social species that isolated living conditions can induce aggression in animals that otherwise would be unlikely to behave that way.

A Drive for Aggression?

In their discussions of aggression among conspecifics, Lorenz (1966) and Eibl-Eibesfeldt (1971) proposed that in natural settings, much aggressive behavior is expressive of an innate drive for aggression that requires frequent dissipation. Under normal circumstances, they hypothesized, this drive is constantly being bled off through the exchange of various species-specific social signals—various threat and/or submission gestures. Among dogs and wolves, for example, the baring of fangs is a threat gesture and moving backwards with tail lowered is a gesture of submission. The exchange of these species-specific social signals presumably dissipates the drive for aggression and prevents the kind of overt violence that would in the long run endanger the survival of that species. A dramatic example of the power of certain species-specific social signals occurs when wolves engage in a battle for dominance. Such battles are violent and blood is often spilled, but they seldom end in death. Just at the point when the dominant animal seems about to tear the loser apart, the loser will throw back its head and bare its throat to the victor. It is as if it has given up and is trying to make the kill as easy as possible. The interesting thing here is that this supreme gesture of submission has exactly the opposite effect. The victor abruptly turns from the loser and calmly walks away, as if its aggressive drive has been turned off completely.

If nature is so arranged that species-specific social signals have the power to dissipate and even to turn off an aggressive drive, then any prolonged failure of an animal to exchange these signals would allow the drive to accumulate to the point at which it will spark an overt attack once a suitable target becomes available. The hypothesis of a drive for aggression and the notion that social signals can dissipate the drive might explain why overt aggression among conspecifics is relatively infrequent and why a period of being isolated would induce an animal to behave aggressively when the opportunity arises.

And so, when our ducklings were housed together there might have been little tendency for any of them to behave aggressively because the drive that supports this behavior was constantly being bled off through exchanges of social signals. When one of these birds was then isolated for a period, its subsequent tendency to attack may have reflected its prior inability to exchange social signals and thereby to bleed off its constantly accumulating drive for aggression.

The theory that aggression is based on a constantly accumulating innate drive seemed to have sufficient explanatory power to account easily for our data. Furthermore, in the works of Lorenz and Eibl-Eibesfeldt, the theory gained widespread acceptance as it was applied (successfully, it seemed) to all sorts of human aggression. Violent spectator sports like football and ice hockey were held to make overt aggression and perhaps even wars less likely. These were but two examples of the many ways that society permits the aggressive drive to bleed off without causing excessive damage. Other examples were to be found not only in all sorts of competitive activities but also in the kinds of violent films and entertainments that were increasingly becoming prevalent.

When I first encountered this line of reasoning, I found it difficult to believe that nature could be arranged in such a way. It implied that organisms actually had a need to be aggressive and that there was little, if anything, to be done about it. Until I had encountered this Lorenzian view, I had thought that aggression was a reaction to particular conditions. I regarded most instances of aggression as either a part of a defensive maneuver or as a response to the frustration engendered by the thwarting of one of the basic needs that animals must satisfy if life is to be sustained. Now, however, I was being told that even if frustration does lead to aggression, there is also a basic need for aggression itself. Furthermore, if this need is not bled off, the inevitable outcome will be overt aggression.

It disturbed me considerably to see our ducklings behaving exactly as would be expected if they were motivated by a strong drive for aggression. They displayed a powerful isolation-induced aggression effect and they did so even when they were placed in the company of ducklings with whom they had formerly lived harmoniously. That the ducklings were only a few days old when this aggression occurred did not help matters. Aggression at an early age was to be expected if this behavior was an expression of an innate genetically determined drive.

I recall that my students and I discussed these observations at length. We found it difficult to believe that our infant ducklings were actually seething bundles of aggression. Finally, one of us (I do not remember who) commented that when we place an animal in isolation, we deprive it of much more than just the opportunity to exchange social signals with conspecifics. We also deprive it of the kinds of reinforcing stimulation that characterize social interactions. That single comment provided the initiative for what I now feel was one of the most informative experiments to come out of our laboratory. We already knew that the stimulation provided by an appropriate imprinting stimulus is reinforcing. We reasoned that if a duckling was permitted the company of an imprinting stimulus during a period of separation from conspecifics, it might not behave aggressively when it returned to its group. This would not necessarily mean that a need for aggression was a figment of the imagination, but it would certainly point to that possibility.

In the experiment we performed to examine this issue (Hoffman, Boskoff, Eiserer, and Klein, 1975), a number of ducklings were hatched in isolation and then socialized to other ducklings by housing them in pairs for the first 24 hours post-hatch. On Day 2, we assigned the birds to experimental conditions as follows: 1) several birds were individually placed in separate housing units, each divided into two sections by a pane of glass. One section was occupied by the duckling and contained its food and water dishes. The other section contained a mechanically operated imprinting stimulus that consisted of a four-inch cube of foam rubber hanging from a string. The pane of glass prevented tactile access to the stimulus while permitting visual contact. Periodic movement of the stimulus was produced by a remote motor that operated for a total of four consecutive hours. Because they received some social stimulation from an imprinting stimulus, we called these birds "partial isolates." 2) A number of other ducklings were placed individually in separate housing units. Each of these units was also divided into two sections by a pane of glass and, as with the partial isolates, the duckling's section contained its food and water dishes. The other section, however, was empty. Because no imprinting stimulus was ever presented to these birds, we called them "total isolates." 3) The rest of the ducklings continued to be housed in pairs, one pair to each of several housing units. We called these birds "nonisolates." Daily 20-minute tests for aggression began after the birds had spent 24 hours in these new housing conditions.

Each of the isolates and partial isolates was tested for aggression eight times. In each test, we placed the duckling in a small arena along with one of the nonisolates and recorded the number of aggressive pecks by each of the two birds. For this purpose, an aggressive peck was defined as a peck by one duckling directed against the other that was of sufficient intensity to elicit an immediate withdrawal reaction.

We found that the isolates emitted an average of just under 30 aggressive pecks per test session, whereas the partial isolates, and the nonisolates that served as targets, averaged less than 14 aggressive pecks per test session. The partial isolates pecked slightly more often than the target birds but in general, their tendency to peck aggressively was much more like that of the target birds than like that of the total isolates.

These results tell us that isolation-induced aggression by ducklings can be largely prevented by housing otherwise isolated ducklings with an imprinting stimulus. In this study, the imprinting stimulus was always behind a pane of glass. This precluded any direct interaction between it and the duckling. Moreover, since the imprinting stimulus consisted of an inanimate block of foam rubber, it could neither make nor respond to the kinds of species-specific social signals that have been proposed to help dissipate a drive for aggression.

Our results provide no comfort for the view of aggression articulated by Lorenz and by Eibl-Eibesfeldt. By preventing isolation-induced aggression even in the absence of exchanges of social signals during isolation, our experiment contradicts the proposition that isolation-induced aggression necessarily reflects an innate drive for aggression. Some aspect of the conditions that ordinarily prevail during a period of isolation must be responsible for the subsequent aggression. If those conditions include exposure to stimulation that elicits filial behavior—for example, an imprinting stimulus, a duckling can experience extended isolation from conspecifics without exhibiting heightened levels of overt aggression. It would seem, therefore, that the critical factor in the isolation-induced aggression we observed was not a lack of opportunity for the isolate to bleed off a growing aggressive drive during its period of isolation; it was the failure to encounter stimulation that elicits filial reactions.

Future research will eventually have to explain why the extended absence of stimulation that elicits filial behavior can lead to aggression. It is possible that this aggression is a reaction to the opponent processes that are hypothesized to become prominent when an affect-arousing stimulus is withdrawn. Could failure to obtain drugs to which an individual has become addicted cause aggressive behavior? It will take specialized research to elucidate the details of such an effect.

13

Social Interactions in the Context of Imprinting

L ike many other animals, including humans, ducklings in a natural setting are often exposed to siblings at the same time that they are becoming socially attached to their mother. In most laboratory settings, on the other hand, the ducklings are housed in isolation before their exposure to the stimulus that is to serve as a maternal surrogate. With the exception of one of our first experiments (Hoffman, 1968) and our studies of aggression (Chapter 12), all of our initial investigations followed this procedure: our birds were hatched and housed in isolation and were individually exposed to the imprinting stimulus.

But we had reasons to suspect that we were missing something. In the one early study in which we had exposed subjects to the imprinting stimulus as a group, the birds attended to each other and appeared largely to ignore the coming and going of the stimulus. We found, however, that when we removed one of those birds from the group, the presentation of the imprinting stimulus suppressed its distress calls in the same fashion as it did for subjects that had been imprinted in isolation. The bird behaved as if imprinting had occurred in the group situation despite the fact that it had appeared there to ignore the stimulus. This finding, in conjunction with our knowledge of what happens in a natural setting, implied that group rearing does not preclude imprinting, but we had yet to focus on the effects of group rearing.

In the first of our studies that were specifically directed at the effects of group rearing (Gaioni et al., 1977), we separated a number of newly hatched ducklings into groups of either ten, six, or three birds. We maintained each group in a separate housing unit where its members had continuous access to food and water as well as to each other. The groups remained intact for a week, after which we systematically removed various numbers of ducklings from each group and measured the distress calling of the remaining birds.

When the groups were intact, the birds seldom sounded distress calls regardless of the size of the group. When, however, various numbers of birds were removed from a group, the fewer that remained, the greater the number of distress calls. Furthermore, a given number of birds remaining from a larger group sounded more distress calls than did the same number of birds remaining from a smaller group. For example, when two birds remained from an original group of three, they gave fewer distress calls than did two birds that remained from an original group of six; these, in turn, gave fewer distress calls than did two birds remaining from an original group of ten. It was as if birds were sensitive to their original group size and as if this sensitivity determined how they would react when their group had been reduced.

Subsequent experiments revealed that neither adding birds to a group nor interchanging birds between groups induced distress calling; hence the distress calling that reductions in group size induced was not simply a reaction to the disappearance of particular individuals or to the stimulus change that necessarily occurred when group size was changed.

We were surprised by this set of results. We had observed previously that ducklings living in pairs rarely, if ever, sounded distress calls unless they were disturbed. If they were separated, however, both birds emitted many distress calls, which persisted until the birds were reunited. Because of the robust nature of this effect, we assumed that even if a duckling was permitted to live in a larger group, the presence of a single companion would, under most circumstances, preclude distress calling. Clearly, we were wrong. Ducklings living in groups are highly stressed by the abrupt disappearance of their companions, and the degree of stress is determined by the number of companions that disappear. The degree of stress is also determined, in part, by the size of the group before the disappearance of those companions.

In addition to revealing something of the richness of our young birds' social interactions, these findings had certain methodological implications. In particular, they told us that if one is assessing the effects of social isolation on an animal's subsequent behavior (as we had done when we were studying aggression), the magnitude of the effects may be influenced by the size of the groups from which the subjects are separated. Fortunately, the effects in our studies of aggression had been quite large, indicating that inadvertently perhaps, we had used groups of an appropriate size. As my former colleague Mike Warren used to say: "Given a choice, it's always better to be lucky than smart."

Once we had ascertained how reductions in group size affected the distress vocalization of group-reared ducklings, we set about to determine how the distress calls of such ducklings would be influenced by the presentation of an appropriate imprinting stimulus. For this research (Gaioni, DePaulo, and Hoffman, 1980), we elected to use the experimenter's hand as the imprinting stimulus because we felt that it might be even more effective than our usual mechanical object. Because we had found (Chapter 7) that older individually reared birds tended to flee an imprinting stimulus, we were especially interested in what would happen when older group-reared birds were first exposed to an imprinting stimulus. Using our hand as the imprinting object would make it possible to track an older bird that was attempting to flee and thus, perhaps, speed the process of "enforced exposure." Also, the experimenter could then provide the ducklings with tactile stimulation. Our mechanical moving object never provided this form of stimulation, yet it is an outstanding element of the variety of stimulation that a mother duck provides in a natural setting. If, as seemed likely, tactile stimulation innately elicits filial reactions in ducklings (presumably, by stimulating the release of endorphins), then a hand might be an especially effective imprinting stimulus. As it turned out, this supposition proved correct.

We formed newly hatched ducklings into groups of 3 or 12. Beginning on Day 1 and continuing to Day 6, we gave the birds in each group two 20- to 30-minute imprinting sessions each day. The experimenter placed his hand in the unit containing the birds and slowly "walked" it about in a more or less haphazard fashion. Whenever his hand touched a duckling or when a duckling approached it, the experimenter gently stroked the bird for a few seconds before continuing his haphazard walk.

Beginning on Day 7, we separated the ducklings into subgroups and assessed the ensuing distress calling. We also determined how the birds' tendency to sound distress calls was influenced by the presentation of the imprinting stimulus— the experimenter's hand. The findings were exactly as before. In addition, the imprinting stimulus strongly controlled the birds' distress calls. We found that: 1) The fewer the ducklings in a subgroup, the more distress calls they gave; 2) a given number of birds separated from a larger group called more often than did an equal number from a smaller group; and 3) regardless of the size of a subgroup or the size of the original group, the ducklings gave fewer distress calls when the imprinting stimulus was present than when it was absent.

A second experiment revealed that when a group of 12 birds that had lived together for five days was first confronted with an imprinting stimulus (again, the experimenter's hand), they reacted with an increase in distress calling and attempted to flee. After several hours of enforced exposure to the stimulus, however, they ceased fleeing from it, began to approach and nuzzle it, and in general, reacted in a filial fashion. All of this replicated our findings with ducklings that had been reared in isolation (Chapter 7). Moreover, when we subsequently reduced group size by splitting the larger group into subgroups, as we had done with the younger birds, the imprinting stimulus exerted a powerful suppressive effect on separation-induced distress calling. All of these findings led us to conclude that social bonds between group-reared ducklings do not preclude the formation of social attachments to an appropriate imprinting object. Also, as with the primary social bond in an isolated duckling, the formation of this bond in group-reared ducklings is not restricted to a brief critical period early in a subject's life. Once again, nature had proved more resilient and more adaptive than had appeared at first glance.

Our earlier work had confirmed that in addition to suppressing distress calls in isolated ducklings, the presentation of an imprinting stimulus can powerfully reinforce ongoing behavior. As we saw in Chapter 2, ducklings will persistently peck at a key when the sole consequence of a peck is brief exposure to an imprinting stimulus that had been present during the first day or so after hatching (during the so-called critical period). As an imprinting stimulus, we had used a moving plastic milk bottle or a moving rectangular block of foam rubber. We wondered if the birds would also peck persistently if, instead of providing for them a brief view of a mechanical imprinting stimulus, we were to arrange for a duckling's pecks to provide a brief view of another duckling. We also wondered if the same effects would obtain when the first exposure to the duckling (as well as to the mechanical stimulus) occurred well after the so called critical period had passed. We had seen that a given imprinting stimulus need not be present during the critical period to suppress distress calling in older ducklings. Would the same hold true of the ability of the stimulus to reinforce ongoing operant behavior, and what seemed equally interesting, would it hold true when that stimulus consisted of another duckling?

To help answer these questions, we hatched a number of ducklings, maintained them in isolation, and then exposed them individually to an imprinting stimulus for several hours on either Day 1 or Day 10 (Gaioni, Hoffman, DePaulo, and Stratton, 1978). For half the ducklings, the imprinting stimulus was the moving block of foam rubber that we had used in our earlier studies. For the rest, it consisted of another duckling that was confined in a small cage located in the center of the compartment that ordinarily housed the mechanical object. When in this cage, the duckling that was to serve as an imprinting stimulus could always see into the continuously illuminated subject compartment, but the subject could only see into the stimulus compartment when that compartment was illuminated.

On the day following exposure to the imprinting stimulus (whether that stimulus was the foam rubber object or another duckling and whether exposure to that stimulus had occurred on Day 1 or Day 10), we attempted to "shape" a key peck by briefly presenting the imprinting stimulus whenever the bird approached the key, and then later, only when it actually pecked the key.

Figure 19 illustrates the results of those efforts. Whether imprinting occurred early or late and whether the imprinting stimulus consisted of the foam rubber object or another duckling, the same pattern emerged. Pecks occurred in bursts separated by intervals when few pecks occurred.

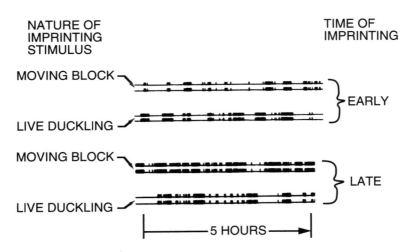

NATURE OF
IMPRINTING
STIMULUS

TIME OF
IMPRINTING

MOVING BLOCK

LIVE DUCKLING

} EARLY

MOVING BLOCK

LIVE DUCKLING

} LATE

├──── 5 HOURS ────►|

Figure 19. Response records for four ducklings (one in each experimental condition). For a given bird, peck responses were reinforced by brief presentation of the indicated imprinting stimulus.

In conjunction with the other findings described earlier in this chapter, this result made it clear that once a duckling begins to react positively to an imprinting object, the entire spectrum of filial reactions is evoked. The object can suppress distress calls and it can reinforce operant behavior. furthermore, subjects tend to respond in bursts. Whether the bird's exposure to the object occurs early or late or whether the object is a mechanical stimulus or another duckling does not seem critical. All of this makes good sense if one assumes a common basis for all of these effects. A good candidate for such a common core is the capacity of the imprinting object to stimulate the subject's production of endorphins.

14

A Conference in Holland

The results of our studies, along with those of a number of other investigators, had provided us with a new way to think about social bonding. Considered together, they pointed to the unexpected conclusion that the bonding process is mediated by the production of endorphins. If we are to understand this process, it will be important to learn as much as possible about the properties and functions of these morphine-like substances. What, exactly, instigates their production? What, exactly, are their behavioral effects? What are their physiological (pharmacological) effects? What happens when their production is terminated? These and numerous other questions readily came to mind as soon as we began to think of social bonding as an addictive process that is mediated by self-produced opiates.

As I contemplated these questions in the 1980's, it became apparent that the answers were not likely to come from the kinds of purely behavioral studies that had led to their formulation. What would be needed, I felt, were studies in which opiates and other physiological variables were directly manipulated, as Panksepp and his colleagues had done in their original work. It became increasingly clear to me that such work had best be left to investigators who, by virtue of their training and inclination, were better equipped than I to engage in these kinds of studies. I felt that although I knew well enough how to carry out behavioral investigations, a full program of research into the neurophysiology of social bonding would require a degree of technical expertise that greatly exceeded my own. Accordingly, in the early 1980's I decided to close down the duckling laboratory.

Many elements, both professional and social, determine the course of a scientist's investigations. The factor that tipped the balance for me at this point was that I felt it was time to focus my attention on a second area of research that had captured my interest years earlier, and on which I and a few of my students had begun work. That research concerned the startle reaction. It had grown out of our discovery that the startle reaction to a sudden explosive sound can be virtually eliminated if a weak, barely audible sound precedes the intense one by about a tenth of a second (Hoffman and Searle, 1965). We called this effect "prepulse inhibition" and began what turned out to be a thirty-year investigation of its basic features.

One day, I hope to write the story of that research endeavor. For now, it may interest those who are curious about scientific progress to hear that a number of years after our initial "discovery" of prepulse inhibition, I was to learn that my friend James Ison at the University of Rochester had independently and almost simultaneously "discovered" the same effect. What is even more interesting, Ison's subsequent historical studies revealed that the effect was originally discovered by Sechenov, a Russian scientist, in 1865. Indeed, over the years, it had been discovered or more properly, rediscovered, at least four times. A few years ago, Jim Ison and I prepared an account of those discoveries and an estimate of their role in the history of psychology (Ison and Hoffman, 1983). In addition to setting the historical record straight, we noted how the phenomenon of prepulse inhibition had come to be confused with classical conditioning. Both involved the presentation of a pair of stimuli and both involved the modification of a reflex. In classical conditioning, however, a reflex that one of the stimuli elicits comes also to be elicited by the other. In prepulse inhibition, a reflex elicited by one stimulus is inhibited by a prior stimulus. That these two behavioral phenomena should be confused at all indicated, we felt, the way one's research interests could reflect the climate of the times. During the brief periods when prepulse inhibition was being studied, interest was so focused on classical conditioning that most researchers failed to notice that they were different phenomena. Our account of the history of prepulse inhibition provides a good example of how research can be affected by popular concerns and the general spirit of the times. I commend it to the interested reader.

In addition to the work on reflex modification, I concentrated my attention on a book on vision and art (Hoffman, 1989) that I had wanted to write for some time. Although I continued to read the research literature on imprinting, I had little contact with workers in this field until I received a letter from Holland indicating that the University of Groningen was about to celebrate its 375th anniversary and that they had decided to host an international conference on imprinting as part of the festivities. They were inviting me to attend.

The conference fit in well with my plans for that summer. As luck would have it, I was at that time already preparing to visit Europe, in part to attend a conference on Vision and Art to be held in Bristol, England, and in part to visit some of the locations in Belgium where I had fought during World War II. A number of years earlier, my wife, Alice, an historian, had undertaken to write a book on memory as it relates to the practice of oral history (Hoffman and Hoffman, 1990). One part of that book was to be a study of my own memories of my experiences as an 18-year-old soldier. When the invitation to Groningen arrived, Alice had finished most of the book and we were planning to find out if a return to the scene of some of the wartime events would stimulate further recollections. It would be easy, therefore, to arrange to attend the conference in Holland and this is what we did.

I have already indicated (Chapter 5) that many discussions at the conference centered on questions about the role of learning in imprinting. Several reports at the conference also dealt with this problem and some of them had a direct bearing on the theoretical interpretation of imprinting that I and one of my students had proposed about fifteen years earlier (Hoffman and Ratner, 1973b).

As noted in Chapter 8, our work had suggested that the learning that occurs in imprinting displays many of the features of the associative processes that Pavlov studied and that had come to be called "classical conditioning." We proposed that the learning in imprinting is an example of this associative process. At Groningen, it was now generally agreed that imprinting was neither instantaneous nor irreversible, and it was the consensus that some form of learning was involved.

Several participants, however, raised some question as to whether classical conditioning was in fact the proper way to describe such learning. There was evidence that mere exposure to a conspicuous stimulus was sufficient for a chick or duckling to begin to react filially and to learn its features. I will have more to say about this in Chapter 17.

Other discussions at the conference concerned the role of a small region in the anterior forebrain roof (the intermediate zone of the medial hyperstriatum ventrali). This brain structure (the IMHV) had been found to be metabolically active during imprinting. At the conference, Gabriel Horn and Patrick Bateson, two of the investigators who, along with Brian McCabe, had participated in this finding (Horn, 1985), described a variety of experiments indicating that destruction of the IMHV can prevent a chick from discriminating between a familiar imprinting stimulus and a novel one but does not prevent that stimulus from continuing to reinforce ongoing responses. I recognized that a dissociation of this sort was consistent with the view of imprinting that our own work had suggested: namely, that imprinting is a process by which the initially neutral features of a stimulus that has other innately reinforcing features acquire the capacity themselves, through a learning process, to reinforce ongoing behavior. Apparently, destruction of the IMHV either prevents this learning or eliminates its effects.

I was gratified by the events at the conference, for although they implied that many important insights were still to be derived from the study of imprinting, much of what we had found had been supported by further investigation. I was especially pleased to observe that by focusing on learning, the newer interpretations of social bonding implied a more forgiving and resilient view of nature than had been postulated by the rigid, implacable notions of imprinting that had dominated the discussions at the earlier conference in England. As a result, I left the conference with a renewed interest in imprinting and with a resolve to set down my thoughts about it one day. My opportunity to do so came several years later when I decided that it was time to retire from the regular teaching faculty at Bryn Mawr College and to assume the role of Professor Emeritus. That same year, I was invited to spend a semester at King's College, Cambridge, where Patrick Bateson was now the Provost and where he and Gabriel Horn were doing their research on imprinting. I had always been impressed by the rigor of their investigations and I saw that a semester at King's would give me an opportunity to bring myself fully up to date on their newest findings. Accordingly, it only took a little while, perhaps 15 seconds, before I began to prepare for that trip.

15

A Term at Cambridge

My stay in Cambridge began in April of 1992. Spring, as the poets say, is a sublime time to be in England. Cambridge, with its ancient buildings, immaculately trimmed lawns, and well tended flower gardens was beautiful beyond description. I cannot imagine a more conducive environment for the kind of intense intellectual activity that has characterized this university. Here were the rooms where Newton penned his laws of motion and Watson and Crick solved the riddle of the double helix. It was no wonder that so much good science had been done here; the setting was perfect.

Shortly after my arrival, I was conducted on a tour of the Sub-Department of Animal Behavior at Madingley, one of the two facilities at Cambridge where research on imprinting is conducted. Madingley consists of a small cluster of research buildings in the middle of some green fields, about five miles from central Cambridge. In addition to providing an excellent setting for the investigation of imprinting in birds, Madingley contains a small laboratory for the scientific investigation of social attachment in human infants. In this work, an infant (with the cooperation of its parents) is placed in a novel setting and its reactions are assessed when one or both of its parents leave the room. The procedures are not unlike those used in research on imprinting.

Madingley also houses a well equipped primate center, with a large outdoor screened enclosure that contains a colony of Rhesus monkeys. The primate facility provided an excellent setting for the study of social development in a species that occupies a niche in the gap between birds and people.

It began to rain fairly hard while I was observing the monkeys as they moved about their enclosure but to my surprise, none of them went inside, although they had only to step through a door to do so. I was told that this was typical of their behavior when it rained. My surprise perhaps indicates the persistence of my tendency toward subjective anthropomorphism despite my best efforts to avoid it. I know that I certainly would have gone indoors to escape the rain.

All in all, Madingley impressed me as a wonderful place to do developmental research. Many others must have felt the same way; the list of scientists who have worked there includes top investigators from all over the world.

Some Differences in Emphasis

The opportunity to view Madingley at first hand was most illuminating, as site visits often are. I had read much of the experimental literature describing the imprinting work that had been done at Cambridge, but it was only after I had visited the facilities there that I became fully aware of the differences and similarities between the work at Cambridge and in my own laboratory.

The differences are numerous, although as will be seen, they are not crucial to the conclusions the work has generated. Some of the imprinting studies at Cambridge used ducklings as subjects but most of that research has been and continues to be conducted with domestic chicks. As in my own laboratory, eggs are hatched in a darkened incubator. In the Cambridge laboratories, however, the chicks are permitted to emerge into a communal setting, although they are quickly separated and placed in individual compartments of a holding incubator where they can hear but not touch or see each other. This procedure differed somewhat from ours. My students and I had always arranged for our ducklings to hatch in auditory, tactual, and visual isolation. We accomplished this by placing a small box over each egg when we first noted the pip marks that indicated that the duckling was beginning to emerge.

Many years ago, my reading of the literature on imprinting had led me to suppose that imprinting might not take place or would be severely impeded if we permitted subjects to interact physically before their first exposure to the imprinting stimulus. Some of the last of our own studies (discussed in Chapter 13) and as will be seen, the ongoing work at Cambridge makes it apparent that this is not necessarily so.

An important difference between the Cambridge laboratories and our own was in the kind of imprinting stimuli they used. Figure 20 shows a few of the stimuli that have served as a mother surrogate for the chicks at Cambridge, and Figure 21 shows some of the test stimuli that have served as alternatives to the jungle fowl that Figure 20 depicts.

Figure 20. Examples of the objects used as imprinting stimuli in the Cambridge laboratories. During stimulus presentation, the object is illuminated and made to rotate. (Adapted from Figure 2.2 in Horn, 1985.)

I show these stimuli to illustrate what I feel is a fundamental difference between the approach of the scientists at Cambridge and my own. Their studies with the stimuli in Figure 20 had revealed that under certain circumstances, the rotating stuffed jungle fowl was more attractive to a chick than the rotating boxes and cylinders. The scrambled objects in Figure 21 were used to identify the visual features of the stuffed jungle fowl that might be responsible for the strong attachment behavior that this object elicited. The cluster of features associated with the head and neck were found to be the critical elements (Johnson and Horn, 1988). In my own work, I had no inclination to use a stuffed duck as an imprinting stimulus largely because the moving block of foam rubber had proved to be adequate for our purposes. Its presentation served as a reinforcer and its withdrawal elicited distress calls. For these reasons and because my interests were

Figure 21. Scrambled versions of the stuffed jungle fowl. (Adapted from Figure 8.12 in Horn, 1985.)

never in ducklings for their own sake, I had no inclination to try to identify an imprinting stimulus that might have been more attractive to them. As an experimental psychologist, I was trying to understand the dynamics of the primary social bond and I was testing ducklings because their behavior seemed likely to tell me something about the nature of that bond. The scientists at Cambridge had broader interests. In addition to their concern for the behavioral dynamics of the primary social bond, they sought to understand its characteristics in natural settings and its neurophysiology.

Another difference between the approach at Cambridge and in my laboratory concerned the degree to which the effects of response contingencies were emphasized. In my laboratory, except when we assessed distress calling as an index of attachment, our studies entailed a specific response contingency: presentation of the imprinting stimulus was contingent on the occurrence of a particular response. Usually, that response was a peck at a key or a pole that hung in the duckling's compartment. In the Cambridge work, stimulus presentation was occasionally contingent on a specific response but most of the time was independent of the subject's overt behavior. Figure 22 shows the experimental arrangement in many of the studies at Cambridge.

Figure 22. An experimental arrangement that has often been used in the Cambridge laboratories. During stimulus presentation, the object is illuminated and rotated. Strength of attachment behavior is indicated by the number of times the wheel is turned as the chick attempts to approach the object. (Adapted from Figure 3.2 in Horn, 1985.)

The chicks were placed in a running wheel and the tendency to run toward or away from the stimulus was assessed. Usually, whether the chick ran toward or away from the stimulus or whether it sat still, it had no effect on the presence or absence of the stimulus. Although distress calling was also assessed at times, interest in most studies was focused on the number of times the wheel rotated as the chick attempted to approach the stimulus.

Imprinting and the Nervous System

A few days after my visit to the Madingley laboratories, I visited the laboratories that are located in the Department of Zoology in the central part of the University. Gabriel Horn, the Chairman of the Department, had previously arranged for this facility to serve as my home base during the several months that my wife and I were to be in Cambridge. Horn and Bateson had done their groundbreaking work on the neurophysiology of imprinting in this facility and it was here that this line of investigation was now being vigorously pursued.

When I arrived, I was invited to observe a test session in which some recently developed techniques were to be used to assess the effects of an imprinting stimulus on the activity of certain brain cells in an imprinted chick. The procedure is called "unit recording." Unit recording had begun to be used in work with cats and monkeys in the 1950's. Since then, it has produced major advances in our knowledge of the organization and functional properties of various aspects of the nervous system. Unit recording in the context of imprinting had been pioneered by Brian McCabe and Gabriel Horn, who anesthetized the chicks during the assessment of their neural activity. More recently however, the procedures had been refined to the point where it was now possible to do unit recording in an unanesthetized, freely moving chick.

The test session I was to observe was to be conducted by Alistair Nicol, a competent young scientist who had begun to work at the laboratory a few months earlier. Approximately 20 hours after it had hatched, the chick that was to be tested had received several hours of exposure to the rotating box shown in Figure 22. Shortly after this training, the chick had been anesthetized and a delicate recording electrode had been surgically inserted into the right side of IMHV. Now (the next day), unit activity was to be recorded while the chick was in the running wheel and was being exposed to the rotating box or to various novel stimuli.

I had been much impressed by the earlier work of the scientists at Cambridge. Now, as I made my way to the room where I was to observe the tests, I found myself thinking that if the recording procedures I was about to witness worked at all, the research at Cambridge would have the potential to revolutionize our understanding of imprinting and perhaps of other important processes such as learning and memory. What concerned me was whether or not the techniques that were needed to do unit recording would interfere with the overt behavior that we had found is ordinarily characteristic of imprinting. I need not have been concerned.

The first thing that struck me when I entered the laboratory was that the chick appeared to have recovered fully from its operation the previous day. Except for the flexible hairlike wire that extended from its head to the recording instruments, the chick looked perfectly normal. It seemed to be in no discomfort at all, acting healthy and alert when tested. It behaved very much like the intact, well-imprinted ducklings I had observed in my own laboratory. During presentation of the rotating box, the bird gave contentment cheeps and attempted to run to the stimulus. Of course, since the chick was in a wheel, these efforts were in vain, but a count of the turns of the wheel provided an index of the strength of its filial reaction. During stimulus withdrawal (accomplished by darkening the stimulus compartment, terminating the box's rotation, and extinguishing its internal lamp), the chick stopped running and began to emit distress calls. I noted, however, that this behavior occurred only after more than three or four seconds of stimulus withdrawal. During brief (less than three seconds) periods of stimulus withdrawal, the bird often continued to run in the direction of the stimulus and continued to emit contentment cheeps.

It was rewarding to observe these features of the bird's behavior. They were almost identical to the way our ducklings had behaved during short versus extended withdrawal of the imprinting stimulus (Chapter 3). Years earlier (Hoffman and Stratton, 1968), we had found that when we divided a given time period into equal cycles of stimulus presentation and withdrawal, the birds gave few if any distress calls when the intervals of stimulus withdrawal were less than five seconds. We had found that when an imprinting stimulus is withdrawn, it usually takes several seconds before a duckling begins to emit distress calls, and that stimulus presentation usually put an immediate end to these calls. Alistair's chick was behaving in exactly the same way.

I was especially pleased to observe these behavioral consistencies. They implied that despite the many differences between procedures at Cambridge and in my laboratory, the two series of investigations had uncovered the same behavioral effects and hence were pointing to the same conclusions about the nature of imprinting. They also implied that the procedures used at Cambridge to assess unit activity were not interfering with the behavior that would ordinarily occur. The chick's reactions during other tests provided further evidence of this proposition. When, for example, a novel rotating cylinder (Figure 20) was substituted for the rotating box, the bird failed to run toward it, and presentation and withdrawal of the rotating cylinder had no effect on distress calling. The chick behaved much like our older ducklings had when they first confronted a novel imprinting stimulus. We had also found that if we required an older duckling to stay in the presence of such a stimulus for a sufficient period, then, rather than reacting with indifference, it began to react in a filial fashion. I asked Alistair if he had observed the same effect when his chicks were repeatedly exposed to a novel imprinting stimulus. He assured me that he had.

Another similarity between the reactions of the chick I was observing and those of our ducklings was revealed when the chick was presented with a sound that had accompanied the initial presentation of the rotating box. Although I had not mentioned this earlier, during those imprinting sessions, the chick always heard the tape-recorded sound of a clucking hen. In the tests described above, however, presentations of the rotating red box were not accompanied by any sounds. But then, in a later test, the imprinting stimulus was removed and the recording of the clucking hen was periodically turned on and off. Whenever the chick heard the sounds, it attempted to run in their direction and began to emit contentment cheeps. Whenever the sounds stopped, the chick stopped running and began distress calling. In essence, the chick behaved in much the same way as our ducklings had behaved when we presented the sound but not the sight of a stimulus to which they had previously been imprinted (Eiserer and Hoffman, 1974). In that study (Chapter 8), when a duckling had been exposed to the sound of the train while viewing the moving imprinting stimulus, subsequent presentation of the sound alone was sufficient to suppress distress calling.

I was interested to learn of similar effects in a study of auditory learning and filial imprinting in the chick (Van Kampen and Bolhuis, 1991). Alistair told me that the sound of a clucking hen had been presented along with the rotating box because doing so tended to enhance the strength of the imprinting bond.

Throughout the session, Alistair had been carefully monitoring the oscilloscope screen that showed the electrical activity of neurons that were responding during presentations of the imprinting stimulus. At one point, about an hour into the session, he commented to me that the results were not exactly as had been anticipated. On the basis of earlier research in the Cambridge laboratories, it was expected that during presentation of the imprinting stimulus, the neural activity in the right IMHV would be relatively low, compared to the high activity levels obtained in previous studies (with other chicks) in which the probe had been located in the left IMHV. This was only the first of the chicks that was to be tested and the recordings had yet to be submitted to the extensive statistical analysis that would be needed to reveal their regularities, but like every good investigator I had known, Alistair had a sense of the character of the recordings as they were arriving; he was expressing his hunch as to what they seemed to be saying.

Shortly after Alistair's comment, we were surprised to discover that the imprinting stimulus seemed to have suddenly lost its capacity to control distress vocalization. As it turned out, however, the problem was with the equipment rather than with the bird. Something had failed in the circuits that controlled stimulus presentation. As a result, the lamps that illuminated the imprinting stimulus were not turning on. The chick's behavior was perfectly consistent. The test, naturally, had to be stopped at this point; it would be continued after the equipment was repaired. Such breakdowns had often happened in my laboratory, too. One can hardly avoid them when working on new problems with newly developed equipment. It was heartening for me and, I suspect for Alistair, too, to realize that when something appeared to be going awry in the experiment, it was the equipment rather than the subject's behavior that was at fault. It reminded me of an important truth I had learned early in my career as a psychologist—behavior is much more reliable than equipment.

I left the laboratory with a feeling of profound respect for the efforts of the scientists at Cambridge. My experiences at Groningen had made it clear that the analysis of imprinting had revealed the phenomenon to be much more plastic and in this sense, forgiving, than its name implies. My own work had pointed in this direction, as had the work in Holland and at Cambridge. What I had just observed was the beginning of a most promising next step. It clearly demonstrated the feasibility of on-line recording from the neural units that mediate imprinting. It seemed to me that in doing so, Horn and his associates at Cambridge had accomplished a major technical achievement.

As my stay in Cambridge progressed, I had other opportunities to observe unit recording in chicks. Each time, the chick's behavior was nearly identical to what I had seen in my ducklings many years before. Consistent with those observations but going a step beyond them, the unit recordings were continuing to indicate that certain of the cells in the IMHV were especially active during the presentation of the stimulus to which the chicks had previously been imprinted. A novel imprinting stimulus, however, had little or no effect on the firing rate of these cells.

In many respects, the activity of these cells was similar to the activity of a now famous brain cell that had been discovered at Princeton University a number of years earlier (Gross, 1972). On that historic occasion, various visual patterns were being focused on the retina of an anesthetized monkey while the investigators assessed unit activity in a brain region known as the inferotemporal cortex. In the course of this work, a cell was found that exhibited a highly specialized function: the only pattern that generated a substantial increase in this cell's activity was an image of a monkey's paw. An image of a square or a star had no effect. An image of a human hand produced some increase in activity but the image of a monkey's paw, with its elongated fingers, produced an enormous increase. Moreover, it mattered little where the image was placed in the monkey's visual field or what its orientation was. It was as if the cell was a part of the brain system where the neural representation of a monkey's paw was processed and/or stored.

The cells that were activated by presenting the imprinting stimulus were similar to the "monkey paw" cell except that cell activity was a product of previous imprinting. To my mind, the most straightforward and economical interpretation of this remarkable finding is that these cells are a part of the neural circuit that is activated during the recognition of a stimulus that the subject has previously encountered. If research continues to support this finding, the Cambridge laboratory will have made a major discovery indeed.

Unit recording was not the only procedure that was used in the Cambridge laboratory during my sojourn there. In an ongoing series of studies, a new biochemical labeling technique was also being used to identify the specific brain cells that are active during a chick's exposure to an imprinting stimulus. This technique also implicated IMHV in the imprinting phenomenon and, what is equally important, was enabling the investigators to visualize some of the spatial relations among the relevant neurons in this brain region.

16

Some Theoretical Comments

In the previous chapter, I noted many similarities between the behavior of the imprinted chicks at Cambridge and of the imprinted ducklings at Bryn Mawr. My tenure at Cambridge provided me with an opportunity to compare my own theoretical interpretation of that behavior with the interpretations of the scientists at Cambridge. I have already indicated some of the ways our interpretations overlapped. We were agreed that imprinting is a more plastic process than its name implies. Imprinting a bird on one stimulus does not necessarily preclude imprinting it on a second stimulus. We were also agreed that imprinting entails a form of more or less gradual learning. That is to say, the process is not an abrupt "stamping in," as its name implies. Finally, we were in agreement that the so-called critical period for imprinting is neither sharply delimited nor critical. Both chicks and ducklings have been imprinted well after the so-called critical period. For this reason, among others, the term "sensitive period" was used at Cambridge to describe the period in a chick's development when imprinting is most readily accomplished.

Our disagreements centered on two theoretical issues: first, we disagreed about the factors responsible for an imprinted bird's avoidance of a novel but otherwise appropriate imprinting stimulus. Second, we disagreed about the nature of the learning that characterizes imprinting.

Is Imprinting a Self-limiting Process?

Consider the factors responsible for an imprinted bird's avoidance of a novel stimulus. Horn (1985) put it this way:

> Such avoidance is a consequence of filial attachment to a particular object: as the chick becomes progressively more familiar with that object it avoids objects that are very different from it. It is as if, once a neural representation of stimulus 1 has been formed, 'not 1' objects are avoided....The developing avoidance behavior could be based on a neural matching system: a strong mismatch between the stored information and the activity evoked in the nervous system by a novel object results in the activation of an avoidance system. (p. 121).

It is, I believe, fair to suggest that this statement implies that mere exposure to an appropriate conspicuous stimulus is sufficient to cause a subject to avoid other conspicuous but distinctive stimuli that would ordinarily have been appropriate for imprinting. In essence, Horn's statement asserts that imprinting is a form of exposure learning and that once this learning has occurred, the process self-terminates.

This interpretation is perfectly consistent with the results of the large number of investigations that had been carried out at the Cambridge laboratories. It differs, however, from the interpretation that my own work had generated. Horn's interpretation left out the role of maturation in the subjects' reactions to novelty. As I noted earlier, my own experiments led me to conclude that the recognition of novelty was only one of the factors that played a role in terminating the sensitive period. The other factor was maturation. If a subject had not matured sufficiently, it might very well be able to recognize that a second imprinting stimulus was novel but still react positively to the second stimulus. This was exactly what my students and I had found two decades earlier (Hoffman and Ratner, 1973a). Those findings had convinced me that a certain amount of maturation is necessary before a duckling (or chick) will fear an otherwise adequate but novel imprinting stimulus.

At the time we carried out that research, we knew that for a newly hatched (17-hour-old) bird, presentation of either our rotating lamp or our moving block of foam rubber would immediately suppress ongoing distress calls. We also knew that unless a duckling had previously seen the stimulus in motion, presentation of that stimulus when it was stationary would not suppress distress calls. What would happen, we wondered, if we were to present one of the stimuli in motion to a young duckling and then observe how its stationary presentation controlled distress calls as compared with stationary presentation of the other stimulus? If only the stimulus previously seen in motion suppressed distress calls, it would mean that the duckling could perfectly well discriminate between the two stimuli. If, in the same session, we then alternated presentations of the two stimuli in motion and found that both stimuli suppressed distress calls, it would mean that despite its having just demonstrated an ability to recognize that the second stimulus was novel, the bird had not yet matured to the point where that novelty could induce sufficient fear to prevent a positive reaction to the stimulus in motion.

Because the results of the experiment were exactly as suggested above and because we had taken care to counterbalance the various conditions, that study provided good evidence that a young duckling's filial reaction to a novel moving stimulus is not based on the bird's inability to recognize that the stimulus is novel. For a young duckling to exhibit fear of an appropriate moving stimulus requires something more than having previously learned the features of some other imprinting stimulus. It requires some maturation.

Findings that I described earlier provide additional evidence for this proposition. Unlike day-old ducklings, ducklings that were five days old reacted fearfully when they first encountered a moving imprinting stimulus (Chapter 2). Furthermore, five-day-old ducklings also reacted fearfully when they first encountered a novel imprinting stimulus after they had previously formed an attachment to some other stimulus (Chapter 7). In both cases, it may be recalled, after sufficient enforced exposure to the new stimulus in motion, the birds became attached to it.

I suspect that a maturational factor in the evolution of a potential attachment object into a fearful object may characterize the developmental process for many organisms. Like ducklings, the young of many other species appear to be responsive to any potential attachment object when they are very little. Every parent knows that anyone can pick up and even comfort an infant when it is very young. At about eight months, however, many infants become quite wary of strangers. Schaffer (1966) provided evidence that such infants can discriminate between their mother and a stranger long before they begin to fear strangers. It may be of interest that in humans, fear of strangers begins to appear at about the time an infant is beginning to become competent at locomotion. In ducklings and chicks, we see the same relation. Fear of novelty begins to become strong at about 48 hours post-hatch, which is close to the time when these birds have started to move about easily.

It is, perhaps, not unreasonable to suppose that a maturational component in fear of novelty would have adaptive value for a species. The capacity of a young organism to react filially to any of a variety of possibly different parents is necessary if it is to survive. The need for some maturation before fear of novelty develops would ensure that the young organism could learn to recognize its parents unencumbered by a fear reaction. The subsequent development of fear of novelty (neophobia) would tend to restrict the filial reaction to the parental figures it had first encountered, usually its biological parents.

I do not assert here that fear of novelty is totally absent in the very young chick or duckling. Rather, I am suggesting that this fear is relatively weak compared to the young subject's readiness to exhibit a filial reaction to an appropriate imprinting stimulus. Seventeen-hour-old ducklings that have never been exposed to an imprinting stimulus sound distress calls when they are first exposed to a new environment, indicating that they recognize novelty. As we saw in Figure 8, however, the initial presentation of a moving imprinting stimulus immediately suppresses these distress calls. This does not happen with older birds. For them, some enforced exposure to a novel imprinting stimulus is required before that stimulus will suppress distress calls.

These observations indicate that the processes responsible for imprinting unfold gradually. It would be incorrect to suppose that there are critical points in the course of maturation where imprinting can or cannot occur.

Exposure Learning versus Classical Conditioning

The only other point of disagreement between my own interpretation of imprinting and that of the scientists at Cambridge centered on our respective accounts of the learning mechanisms that we ascribe to the process. At Cambridge, imprinting was viewed as a form of perceptual or exposure learning in which the critical event is the subject's exposure to the imprinting stimulus during the sensitive period.

A paper from the Cambridge laboratories discussed this "exposure learning" view of imprinting in some detail (Hollis, ten Cate, and Bateson, 1991). It described the theoretical model of imprinting that Bateson developed in the early 1980's and that was later elaborated to the point where it makes testable quantitative predictions (Bateson, 1990, 1991). Bateson's theory postulates that primarily through repeated exposure, a chick or duckling forms a neuronal representation of an imprinting stimulus. The basic idea is that the subject's nervous system analyzes the input to its receptors in terms of the specific feature detectors that have been activated and in terms of how often

158

various detectors have been activated at the same time. In this context, a feature detector is conceived to be an assembly of neurons that is activated by a given feature of the imprinting stimulus like its particular shape, size, or color. Hollis et al. (1991) described their conception of what happens as follows:

> ...the analyzing system decomposes input into its features, preserving information about the intensity with which each of the feature detectors has been activated. Each of these feature detectors is connected to a separate population of neurons in the recognition system. Repeated exposure to an imprinting object results in the strengthening of connections between particular feature detectors activated by that object and a subset of neurons in the recognition system. These strengthened connections constitute the representation of the imprinting object. (p. 309).

The formation of a neural representation of the imprinting object is not the only process in the theoretical account of imprinting that Bateson and his coworkers developed. It was, however, conceived to be a direct consequence of exposure to an imprinting stimulus and was postulated to be the key mechanism through which a subject forms an internal representation of an imprinting stimulus and thus recognizes it on future occasions. It was also proposed that the formation of this representation is a sufficient condition for the subject subsequently to avoid a reasonably novel imprinting stimulus.

The perceptual learning described by Hollis et al. provides a nervous-system mechanism that would permit a chick or duckling's various encounters with an imprinting stimulus to form a single internal representation so that the stimulus will be recognized on future occasions. Missing, however, is an account of why a chick or duckling should exhibit an immediate filial reaction to certain especially effective imprinting stimuli. I have proposed that this happens because certain features of the stimulus innately elicit filial behavior. For a chick or duckling, a stimulus configuration that serves this purpose is its natural parent. The research in my laboratory suggests that for ducklings, seeing the mother in motion is an important component of that configuration. The studies by Johnson and Horn that I discussed earlier suggest that the configuration of the mother's head and neck is another such component.

If a chick or duckling is to recognize an imprinting object to which it has previously been exposed, it must form some kind of neuronal representation of that object. In addition to recognizing its original imprinting stimulus, however, a chick or duckling must also react filially when its view of the stimulus fails to include the specific features that innately elicited the filial reaction. For example, there are times when a chick or duckling's mother is stationary and is not showing her head and neck. It could be important for the filial reaction to continue even at such times. I have suggested that this continued reaction is an example of a conditioned response and that it is a product of classical conditioning.

More specifically, I have proposed that during its initial exposure to an imprinting stimulus, the subject acquires a conditioned filial reaction to features that will make the stimulus recognizable in other circumstances but that do not themselves initially elicit a filial reaction. Presumably, this happens because these features have been consistently presented in close temporal and spatial contiguity with the features of the imprinting stimulus that do innately elicit a filial reaction. This classical conditioning process is assumed to be mediated by the production of endorphins, and the social interaction that results is assumed to involve some form of opponent process, as Solomon and Corbit (1974) postulated.

The proposition that imprinting involves a form of perceptual or exposure learning is thus not wrong in my view; rather, it is incomplete. This having been said, I must note that I feel that the differences in the interpretations offered by the scientists at Cambridge and myself reflect what we have elected to emphasize in our investigations and writings, rather than differences in our fundamental viewpoints. Furthermore, it seems reasonable to suppose that as research on imprinting continues, these differences, such as they are, will gradually be resolved. For example, our differences with respect to the role of maturational factors in fear of novelty is clearly an empirical issue and in the long run, will have to be resolved in the laboratory. In science, unlike some other aspects of human endeavor, the final arbiter will be data that one or another decisive experiment generates. In a like manner, our theoretical differences will eventually be resolved as the laboratory analysis of imprinting continues to provide data with new and perhaps unanticipated twists. It is in the nature of most scientific theory that it is continuously refined and expanded to accommodate the data that new research generates.

Bateson designed his theory to account for how a chick or duckling forms an internal representation of a particular imprinting stimulus and how, having done so, it will exhibit a preference for that stimulus over a novel stimulus that might initially have been equally or even more attractive (Bateson, 1990, 1991). As noted earlier, this theory does not incorporate a maturational factor to account for fear of novelty. Nor does it include a learning process by which the initially neutral features of an imprinting stimulus could themselves come to elicit filial reactions. This does not mean, however, that the theory is incapable of ever accommodating these processes.

It is, I think, relevant that in one of our conversations, Bateson told me that for the sake of theoretical parsimony, he had assumed that the separate features of an imprinting stimulus made equal contributions to the recognition process. Ever since Occam elaborated his law of parsimony in the middle ages, scientists have recognized that a simple theory is the most amenable to experimental test. Theory that incorporates complex multiple ideas too often introduces error and cannot be voted up or down by the results of experiment. Therefore, Bateson's desire to keep his theory as simple as possible is understandable. He also told me, however, that if the data should demand it, the theory would require only a small change to accommodate the fact that some features of a stimulus are more effective in eliciting filial behavior than others.

In that same conversation, Bateson also discussed the role of maturation in imprinting as it related to his theoretical model. In his model, it is the development of inhibitory connections that leads to fear of novelty. Bateson thought that the contribution of maturation to fear of novelty might be especially difficult to determine experimentally if, as his model assumes, the formation of inhibitory connections proceeds rather slowly during exposure to an imprinting stimulus. Under such circumstances, exposure duration would in most instances be necessarily confounded with maturation. He added, however, that although his present model was proving adequate to account for most of the current laboratory findings, if it should fail to do so in the future, he would have no hesitation about modifying it. It is, I think, greatly to Bateson's credit that like every first rate scientist I have known, his theorizing is completely data driven. Hence, he is fully open to whatever new lessons the laboratory might provide.

17

Another Chance Encounter

In Chapter 10, I described how a chance encounter with Richard Solomon led to the resolution of the mystery of why ducklings peck for an imprinting stimulus in bursts and to my conclusion that social attachment is an addictive process mediated by the endorphins. Another chance encounter at Cambridge was to strengthen that conclusion and reveal some of the details of how the endorphins produce their effects.

About six weeks before my departure from Cambridge, I was scheduled to present an account of my research to the scientists at Madingley. I had been asked to give this talk shortly after my arrival in Cambridge. A few days later, I was asked to provide a title so that the presentation could be properly advertised. I was told that the topic was up to me, and after a moments of thought, I suggested that since I had done my work on imprinting many years ago, it might be best if I spoke about my more recent research on the blink reflex in newborn human infants. It was agreed that this topic would surely be of interest to the scientists at Madingley, so I provided a title and thought no more about it until I started to arrange my slides a few days before I was to deliver the talk. As I was picking out my slides, my wife commented that because imprinting was still being studied at Madingley, it might be a good idea to explain why I had stopped my own investigations on this topic. I agreed, and when I introduced my talk, I read the paragraphs in Chapter 14 in which I explained that once I had concluded that social attachment was mediated by the endorphins, I also concluded that the most productive direction for future investigations would be studies in which these opiates and other physiological variables were directly manipulated. I went on to note that I felt that such investigations had best be left to scientists who were better qualified than I to manipulate these variables. I then called for the first slide and launched into my presentation on the infant blink reflex.

Judging from the lengthy discussion it generated, the talk seemed to have been well received. After I gathered up my slides and was walking out of the building, one of the scientists from the audience, Eric Keverne, approached me and asked if I knew about the research on endorphins that was being conducted at Madingley. I was astounded by his question because I had toured the Madingley laboratories shortly after my arrival at Cambridge and none of my escorts had mentioned this work, even though my views about the role of endorphins in imprinting were known to them. My surprise must have been quite evident because, when I responded in the negative, my questioner offered to provide me immediately with reprints of that work and went to his rooms to obtain them.

In retrospect, it is easy to understand why I had not been informed of Keverne's work either during my initial tour of Madingley or during my discussions at the Zoology department. None of the scientists I spoke to at either location had heard about this research or, if they had, they had not associated it with their own work on imprinting. The reason is now clear: the research on endorphins was being conducted with primates; the research on imprinting, with birds. It is easy to understand why investigators working with such different species might not be up-to-date on each other's findings.

There was a lesson in this observation. In spite of all of our conferences and discussions, in spite of all of our networking and publication, it does happen that scientists working in close proximity to one another can fail to see connections between their research interests and thus lose the opportunity to gain the breadth of outlook that inter- and intradisciplinary communication can sometimes induce.

Later, when I began to study the reprints Keverne had given me, I must have uttered a private word of thanks for the good fortune my chance encounter with him had bestowed on me. Had my wife not suggested that I explain to my audience why I was not talking about imprinting, I would never have mentioned endorphins in my talk and would probably have left Cambridge without ever learning of the work of Keverne and his colleagues in the primate facility. Not only had this work demonstrated an effect of endorphins on the social behavior of primates, but it had begun to explain the neural basis for this effect.

The primate studied by Keverne and his associates (Keverne, Martensz, and Tuite, 1989) was the rather diminutive talapoin monkey that is native to the rain forest of West Africa. In an investigation spanning more than a dozen years, several experimental groups of three to five adult monkeys were observed for 50 minutes twice a day, with all animals monitored for social interactions. In addition, a sequence of experiments was performed in which pairs of animals that were housed separately were reunited for 15 minutes every other day. Each animal in a pair was observed when with its partner (on even days) and when isolated (on the other days). Shortly after each observation session, a small sample of cerebrospinal fluid was collected under ketamine anesthesia. These samples were analyzed to determine the amounts of endorphin they contained, and these amounts were found to be related to the behavior that had been recorded during the previous observation session.

Subsequent experiments followed the same basic procedure except that immediately before each observation period, one of the animals in a pair was injected with morphine, a drug that increased the amount of circulating opiates, or with naloxone, a drug that blocked the effects of opiates. On these days, the other animal in the pair received a placebo.

It is beyond the scope of this book to describe the details of the findings. Certain of their basic features, however, are directly relevant to the results of experiments performed in my laboratory with ducklings and to the conclusions about the addictive character of social interactions that my students and I derived from them.

The most relevant findings concerned the relation between the tendency of the monkeys to groom themselves and each other and the amount of endorphins in their cerebrospinal fluid. In essence, it was found that grooming initiated the production of endorphins; when groomed by another monkey during the few minutes of social contact permitted every other day, the groomed monkeys exhibited a large increase in endorphins in their cerebrospinal fluid. Furthermore, the prior administration of morphine reduced the amount of grooming, whereas the prior administration of naloxone enhanced grooming and increased the number of invitations to be groomed. Keverne et al. (1989) concluded that their findings "...support the view that brain opioids play an important role in mediating social attachment and may provide the neural basis on which primate society has evolved." (p. 155).

A more recent publication by Keverne (1992) discusses these findings and relates them to some of the ways the brain's opioids influence and are influenced by social attachment. He notes:

> ...there is an increasing amount of data implicating endorphin in early social bonding of mother and infant in a wide variety of mammals (cat, dog, guinea pig). Parturition, an event of importance to the immediate onset of maternal behavior in rodents and mother/infant selective bonding in sheep has been shown to increase endorphin levels in the limbic brain. (p.23).

Keverne also notes:

> Feeding behavior has been reported to increase during acute infusions of morphine or endorphin into amygdala (central nucleus), hypothalamus (ventromedial nucleus), or the accumbens, whereas naloxone decreases feeding when given centrally. (p. 23).

Finally, Keverne has this to say about the role of endorphins in social attachment as it relates to grooming in primates:

Increased grooming and grooming invitations normally occur in pair bonding of primates during and following copulation, in cementing social relationships, particularly between mothers and infants, and following aggressive outbursts. Grooming interactions form part of the normal behavioral repertoire of primates, occurring in different social situations and having in common the provision of bonding and comfort to the participants rather than being purely hygienic. It therefore appears that grooming is a significant proximate factor in social bonding and for activating the brain's opioid system, as can be seen from the rapid increase in endorphin contingent on receiving grooming. Hence, at the neural level the brain's endorphin system may provide the basis for a common bonding mechanism, but the nature of the relationships clearly differ (Mother/infant; consortships; peers). Nevertheless, it is surely no coincidence that in primates all of these relationships share a strong mutual grooming component. (p. 25).

There are many opportunities here for some exciting research. For example, I would add to Keverne's comments that if our findings with ducklings have application to primates (and I believe they do), grooming is not the only avenue through which social interaction can initiate the production of endorphins. I would suspect that through their association with the stimulation provided by grooming, the sight and sounds of the social partner would themselves eventually acquire this important capacity. An associative learning mechanism of this sort can account for the finding that the sight of a soft claspable object encased in a plastic box can suppress the distress cries of an infant monkey, once the monkey has had sufficient opportunity to climb on and otherwise make tactile contact with the object (Mason, Hill, and Thompson, 1971). As was noted in Chapter 8, an associative learning mechanism of this sort can also account for the finding that a stationary imprinting stimulus can suppress the distress calls of a newly hatched duckling, once the duckling has had sufficient exposure to the stimulus in motion.

18

A Look To the Future

The research at Cambridge seemed to me on the verge of a major breakthrough in the analysis of how the brain is organized to recognize a previously encountered stimulus. I found this a most exciting prospect. In my view, however, there are even more exciting prospects in the research that will surely follow. In it, the aspects of social attachment reflected in the actions of the endorphins will be investigated in a manner comparable to the way the internal representation of the imprinting stimulus is being sought.

It may turn out that these two aspects of social attachment are processed by different neural systems with different locations in the brain. If this is so, it will be important to identify the sites of their actions and to determine how they combine to shape the course of social attachments. I can think of no setting better suited than Cambridge to weave together the separate strands of this complex story. In addition to housing facilities in which both sides of the attachment phenomenon are being investigated, albeit independently, Cambridge is a center that has already made considerable progress on the theoretical side of its interpretation. Bateson's quantitative model of imprinting has been elaborated to the point where it now makes testable predictions about the capacity of a chick to recognize an imprinting stimulus after various amounts of exposure to it (Bateson, 1990, 1991). Although the theory concerns itself primarily with data generated in ongoing investigations of the neurobiology of recognition, there is no reason why it could not be expanded to deal also with the kind of motivational processes that Keverne and I have investigated. Perhaps some version of opponent process theory could be interlaced with a revised version of Bateson's theory to achieve this end. Such an expanded theory could, in principle, provide the kind of conceptual framework that seems needed to deal with the varied behavioral effects that characterize social attachments. In Chapter 6, I described some of our findings about the way presentation of the imprinting stimulus induces a duckling to eat. The recent findings that Keverne described on the effects of opiates and naloxone on feeding behavior are clearly consistent with our behavioral observations and are also consistent with the interpretations that opponent process theory suggests. What seems needed now is a new theoretical structure that will accommodate all these issues

In a similar vein, it will be important to pursue possible links that our research with ducklings has suggested between aggressive behavior and the production of endorphins. Again, what seems needed is a theoretical framework that will make it possible to integrate what initially appeared to be fragmentary and diverse observations.

It will also be important for any reasonably comprehensive theoretical account of imprinting to accommodate the potent classical conditioning effects that characterize this phenomenon. Such effects must play an important role in most if not all of the social behavior that imprinting engenders. Earlier, I described Keverne's finding that in primates, grooming can instigate the production of endorphins. I voiced my suspicion that there is probably an important conditioning component to this effect. Although it seems likely that certain aspects of the social stimulation involved in grooming have an innate capacity to initiate the production of endorphins, it is also possible that other aspects acquire this capacity through their prior association with the endorphin-instigating maternal stimulation that a primate ordinarily receives in the course of its development. The possible role of early conditioning in the production of endorphins that grooming engenders is open to experimental analysis, and the existence of a well articulated theory of imprinting would be helpful in guiding that research.

Finally, there is another reason why an expanded theory of imprinting seems called for in the near future. The evidence is quite clear that the social attachment engendered by imprinting has many if not all of the features of an addiction. For this reason, it will be important eventually to integrate what is known about imprinting with what is known about addictions. This will be no small task.

For example, there is an extraordinary set of findings with respect to the conditioning effects that occur with the taking of narcotics. Over the years, those findings pointed to the conclusion that during drug self-administration, the stimulation from the setting where one takes the drug comes to inhibit the response that the drug ordinarily elicits. It is as if these stimuli come to evoke a conditioned opponent process. The scientist who conducted this research, Shepard Siegel, concluded that this conditioned inhibitory effect is probably responsible for the reduced high that a given dose of a narcotic comes to produce in an experienced addict (Siegel et al., 1982). Siegel also deduced, however, that if this is so, then there might be a tendency for addicts to overdose (and die) if they self-administered their customary dose in a novel setting. This might happen because the new setting would not inhibit the drug response. When he examined the overdose reports, it turned out that this often happened—the overdose had been taken in a new environment. To nail the issue down, Siegel permitted rats to repeatedly self-administer morphine until they had established a customary dosage. He then changed the animals' cages so as to remove the cues that he suspected had come to suppress their response to the drug. The animals proceeded to self-administer their usual dosage, but now, in the absence of the inhibitory cues, that dose was too high: most of them succumbed.

Opponent process theory may prove helpful in integrating the findings on addictions and social attachment. If that theory does not succeed, some other kind of organized conceptual structure will be needed to integrate the myriad of complex effects that arise from the interface between addictions and social attachments. I suspect that such a structure is likely to be developed at Cambridge.

References

Barrett, J. E. (1972). Schedules of electric shock presentation in the behavioral control of imprinted ducklings. *Journal of the Experimental Analysis of Behavior,* **18,** 305-321.

Barrett, J. E., Hoffman, H. S., Stratton, J. W. & Newby, V., (1971). Aversive control of following in imprinted ducklings. *Learning and Motivation,* **2,** 202-203.

Bateson, P. P. G. (1964). Changes in chicks' responses to novel moving objects over the sensitive period for imprinting. *Animal Behaviour,* **12,** 479-489.

Bateson, P. P. G. (1971). Imprinting. In H. Moltz (Ed.), *The ontogeny of vertebrate behavior.* New York: Academic Press.

Bateson, P. P. G. (1990). Is imprinting such a special case? *Philosophical Transactions of the Royal Society, London,* **329,** 125-131.

Bateson, P. P. G. (1990). Obituary (Konrad Lorenz). *American Psychologist,* **45,** 65-66.

Bateson, P. P. G. (1991). Making sense of behavioural development in the chick. In R. J. Andrews (Ed.), *Neural and behavioural plasticity: The use of the domestic chick as a model* (pp. 157-159). London: Oxford University Press.

Blakemore, C., & Cooper, G. F. (1970). Development of the brain depends on the visual environment. *Nature,* **228,** 477-478.

Bloom, B. S. (1964). *Stability and change in human characteristics.* London: John Wiley & Sons.

Candland, D. K., & Campbell, B. A. (1962). Development of fear in the rat as measured by behavior in the open field. *Journal of Comparative and Physiological Psychology,* **55,** 593-596.

Conant, J. B. (1951). *Science and common sense.* New Haven: Yale University Press.

Cynader, M., & Chernenko, G. (1976). Abolition of directional selectivity in the visual cortex of the cat. *Science,* **193,** 504-505.

DePaulo, P. & Hoffman, H. S. (1980). The temporal pattern of attachment behavior in the context of imprinting. *Behavioral and Neural Biology,* **28,** 48-64.

Eibl-Eibesfeldt, I. (1971). *Love and hate: The natural history of behavior patterns* (G. Strachan, Trans.). New York: Holt, Rinehart, & Winston.

Eiserer, L., & Hoffman, H. S. (1974). Acquisition of behavioral control by the auditory features of an imprinting object. *Animal Learning and Behavior,* **2,** 275-277.

Freeman, R. D., Mitchell, D. E., & Millodot, M. A. (1972). Neural effect of partial visual deprivation in humans. *Science,* **175,** 1384-1386.

Gaioni, S. J., DePaulo, P., & Hoffman, H. S. (1980). Effects of group rearing on the control exerted by an imprinting stimulus. *Animal Learning and Behavior,* **8,** 673-678.

Gaioni, S. J., Hoffman, H. S., DePaulo, P., Stratton, J. W., & Newby, V. (1978). Imprinting in older ducklings: Some tests of a reinforcement model. *Animal Learning and Behavior,* **6,** 19-26.

Gaioni, S. J., Hoffman, H. S., Klein, S. H., & DePaulo, P. (1977). Distress calling as a function of group size in newly hatched ducklings. *Journal of Experimental Psychology: Animal Behavior Processes,* **3,** 335-342.

Gottlieb, G. (1965). Imprinting in relation to parental and species identification by avian neonates. *Journal of Comparative and Physiological Psychology,* **59,** 345-356.

Gray, P. H., & Howard, K. I. (1957). Specific recognition of humans in imprinted chicks. *Perception and Motor Skills,* **7,** 301-304.

Gross, C. G., Rocha-Miranda, C. E., & Bebder, D. B. (1972). Visual properties of neurons in inferotemporal cortex of the Macaque. *Journal of Neurophysiology,* **35,** 96-111.

Hafez, E. S. E. (1958). *The behavior of domestic animals.* London: Bailliere.

References

Harlow, H. F. (1974). *Learning to love*. New York: J. Aronson.

Harlow, H. F., & Yudin, H. C. (1933). Social behavior of primates. I: Social facilitation of feeding in the monkey and its relation to attitudes of ascendence and submission. *Journal of Comparative Psychology*, **16**, 171-185.

Hart, B. M., Allen, K. E., Buell, J. S., Harris, F. R., & Wolfe, M. M. (1964). Effects of social reinforcement on operant crying. *Journal of Experimental Child Psychology*, **1**, 145-153.

Herman, B. H., & Panksepp, J. (1978). Evidence for opiate mediation of social affect. *Pharmacology, Biochemistry and Behavior*, **9**, 213-220.

Hersher, L., Richmond, J. B., & Moore, A. V. (1963). Modifiability of the critical period for the development of maternal behavior in sheep and goats. *Behaviour*, **20**, 311-320.

Herzog, H. A. (1988). The moral status of mice. *American Psychologist*, **43**, 473-474.

Hess, E. H. (1957). Effects of meprobamate on imprinting in water fowl. *Annals of the New York Academy of Sciences*, **7**, 724-732.

Hess, E. H. (1959a). Two conditions limiting critical age of imprinting. *Journal of Comparative and Physiological Psychology*, **52**, 515-518.

Hess, E. H. (1959b). Imprinting. *Science*, **130**, 133-141.

Hess, E. H. (1973). *Imprinting: Early experience and the developmental psychology of attachment*. New York: Van Nostrand Reinhold Co.

Hickey, T. L. (1977). Postnatal development of the human lateral geniculate nucleus: Relationship to a critical period for the visual system. *Science*, **198**, 836-838.

Hinde, R. A. (1955). The following response of moor hens and coots. *British Journal of Animal Behaviour*, **3**, 121-122.

Hinde, R. A., Thorpe, W. H., & Vince, M. A. (1956). The following response of young coots and moor hens. *Behaviour*, **11**, 214-242.

Hoffman A. M., & Hoffman H. S. (1990). *Archives of memory: A soldier recalls World War II*. Lexington, KY: University Press of Kentucky.

Hoffman, H. S. (1968). The control of distress vocalization by an imprinted stimulus. *Behaviour, 30,* 175-191.

Hoffman, H. S. (Producer and Director). (1970). *Social reactions in imprinted ducklings* [Film]. (Available from The Psychological Cinema Register, Pennsylvania State University, University Park, PA.)

Hoffman, H. S. (1989). *Vision and the art of drawing.* Englewood Cliffs, NJ: Prentice Hall.

Hoffman, H. S., Boskoff, K. J., Eiserer, L. A., & Klein, S. H. (1975). Isolation-induced aggression in newly-hatched ducklings. *Journal of Comparative and Physiological Psychology, 89,* 447-457.

Hoffman, H. S., Eiserer, L. A., Ratner, A. M., & Pickering, V. L. (1974). Development of distress vocalization during withdrawal of an imprinting stimulus. *Journal of Comparative and Physiological Psychology, 86,* 563-568.

Hoffman, H. S., Eiserer, L. A., & Singer, D. (1972). Acquisition of behavioral control by a stationary imprinting stimulus. *Psychonomic Science, 26,* 146-148.

Hoffman, H. S., & Kozma, F. (1967). Behavioral control by an imprinting stimulus: long-term effects. *Journal of the Experimental Analysis of Behavior, 10,* 495-501.

Hoffman, H. S., & Ratner, A. M. (1973a). Effects of stimulus and environmental familiarity on visual imprinting in newly hatched ducklings. *Journal of Comparative and Physiological Psychology, 85,* 11-19.

Hoffman, H. S., & Ratner, A. M. (1973b). A reinforcement model of imprinting: Implications for socialization in monkeys and men. *Psychological Review, 80,* 527-544.

Hoffman, H. S., Ratner, A. M., & Eiserer, L. A. (1972). Role of visual imprinting in the emergence of specific filial attachment in ducklings. *Journal of Comparative and Physiological Psychology, 81,* 399-409.

Hoffman, H. S., Schiff, D., Adams, J., & Searle, J. (1966). Enhanced distress vocalization through selective reinforcement. *Science, 151,* 352-354.

Hoffman, H. S., & Searle, J. L. (1965). Acoustic variables in the modification of the startle reflex in the rat. *Journal of Comparative and Physiological Psychology, 60,* 53-58.

Hoffman, H. S., Searle, J. L., Toffee, S., & Kozma, F. (1966). Behavioral control by an imprinting stimulus. *Journal of the Experimental Analysis of Behavior, 9,* 179-189.

References

Hoffman, H. S., & Stratton, J. (1968). Schedule factors in the emission of distress calls. *Psychonomic Science*, **10**, 251-252.

Hoffman, H. S., Stratton, J. W., & Newby, V. (1969). The control of feeding behavior by an imprinting stimulus. *Journal of the Experimental Analysis of Behavior*, **12**, 847-860.

Hoffman, H. S., Stratton, J. W., & Newby, V. (1969). Punishment by response-contingent withdrawal of an imprinting stimulus. *Science*, **163**, 702-704.

Hoffman, H. S., Stratton, J. W., Newby, V., & Barrett, J. E. (1970). Development of behavioral control by an imprinting stimulus. *Journal of Comparative and Psysiological Psychology*, **2**, 229-236.

Hollis, K. L., ten Cate, C., & Bateson, P. (1991). Stimulus representation: A subprocess of imprinting and conditioning. *Journal of Comparative Psychology*, **105**, 307-317.

Horn G. (1985). *Memory, imprinting and the brain.* Oxford: Clarendon Press.

Hubel, D. H., & Wiesel, T. N. (1970). The period of susceptibility to the physiological effects of unilateral eye closure in kittens. *Journal of Physiology*, **206**, 419-436.

Hull, C. L. (1943). *Principles of behavior.* New York: Appleton-Century-Crofts.

Ison, J. R., & Hoffman, H. S. (1983). Reflex modification in the domain of startle: II. The anomalous history of a robust and ubiquitous phenomenon. *Psychological Bulletin*, **94**, 3-17.

Jacob, F. (1977). Evolution and tinkering. *Science*, **196**, 1161-1166.

Jaynes, J. (1957). Imprinting: The interaction of learned and innate behavior: II. The critical period. *Journal of Comparative and Physiological Psychology*, **50**, 6-10.

Jaynes, J. (1958). Imprinting: The interaction of learned and innate behavior: III. Generalization and emergent discrimination. *Journal of Comparative and Physiological Psychology*, **51**, 234-237.

Johnson, M. H., & Horn, G. (1988). Development of filial preferences in dark reared chicks. *Animal Behaviour*, **36**, 1000-1006.

Keverne, E. B. (1992). Primate social relationships: Their determinants and consequences. *Advances in the Study of Behavior,* **21,** 1-37. New York: Academic Press.

Keverne, E. B., Martensz, N. D., & Tuite, B. (1989). Beta-endorphin concentrations in cerebrospinal fluid of monkeys are influenced by grooming relationships. *Psychoneuroendocrinology,* **14,** 155-161.

Klaus, M. H., & Kennell, J. H. (1976). *Maternal-infant bonding.* St. Louis, MO: Mosby.

Klaus, M. H., & Kennell, J. H. (1982). *Parent-infant bonding.* St. Louis, MO: Mosby.

Kovach, J. K., & Hess, E. H. (1963). Imprinting: Effects of painful stimulation upon the following response. *Journal of Comparative and Physiological Psychology,* **56,** 461-464.

Lorenz, K. (1935). Der kumpan in der umwelt des vobels [The companion of the bird in its environment]. *Journal of Ornithology,* **83,** 137-213.

Lorenz, K. (1966). *On aggression* (M. K. Wilson, Trans.). New York: Bantam Books. (Original work published 1963).

Mason, W. A., Hill, S. D., & Thompson, C. E. (1971). Perceptual factors in the development of filial attachment. *Proceedings of the 3rd International Primatological Congress,* **3,** 125-133.

Mason, W. A., & Kenney, M. D. (1974). Redirection of filial attachments in rhesus monkeys: dogs as mother-surrogates. *Science,* **183,** 1209-1211.

Mitchell, D. E., Freeman, R. D., Millodot, M., & Haegerstrom, G. (1973). Meridional amblyopia: Evidence for modification of the human visual system by early visual experience. *Vision Research,* **13,** 535-558.

Moltz, H., Rosenblum, L. A., & Halikas, N. (1959). Imprinting and level of anxiety. *Journal of Comparative and Physiological Psychology,* **52,** 240-244.

Moore, D. J., & Shiek, P. (1971). Toward a theory of early infantile autism. *Psychological Review,* **78,** 451-456.

Myers, B. J. (1987). Mother infant bonding as a critical period. In Bornstein, M. (Ed.), *Sensitive periods in development* (pp. 223-245). New Jersey: Lawrence Erlbaum.

Panksepp, J., Vilberg, T., Bean, N. J., Coh, D. H., & Kastin, A. J. (1978). Reduction of distress vocalization in chicks by opiate-like peptides. *Brain Research Bulletin,* **3,** 663-667.

References

Peterson, N. (1960). Control of behavior by presentation of an imprinting stimulus. *Science,***132**, 1295-1296.

Rajecki, D. W. (1973). Imprinting the precocial birds: Interpretation, evidence, and evaluation. *Psychological Bulletin,* **79,** 48-58.

Ramsay, A. O., & Hess, E. H. (1954). A laboratory approach to the study of imprinting. *Wilson Bulletin,* **66,** 196-206.

Ratner, A. M. (1976). Modification of ducklings' filial behavior by aversive stimulation. *Journal of Experimental Psychology: Animal Behavior Processes,* **2,** 266-284.

Ratner, A. M., & Hoffman, H. S. (1974). Evidence for a critical period for imprinting in Khaki Campbell ducklings (Anas platyrhynchos domesticus). *Animal Behaviour,* **22,** 249-255.

Ratner, S. C., & Thompson, R. W. (1960). Immobility reactions (fear) of domestic fowl as a function of age and prior experience. *Animal Behaviour,* **8,** 186-191.

Ross, S., & Ross, J. G. (1949). Social facilitation of feeding behavior in dogs. II: Feeding after satiation. *Journal of Genetic Psychology,* **74,** 293 - 304.

Schaffer, H. R. (1966). The onset of fear of strangers and the incongruity hypothesis. *Journal of Child Psychology and Psychiatry,* **7,** 95-106.

Schein, M. W., & Hale, E. B. The effect of early social experience on male sexual behavior of androgen injected turkeys. *Animal Behaviour,* **7,** 189-200.

Scott, J. P. (1968). *Early experience and the organization of behavior.* Belmont, CA: Wadsworth.

Siegel, S., Hinson, R. E., Krank, M. D., & McCully, J. (1982). Heroin "overdose death": Contribution of drug-associated environmental cues. *Science,* **216,** 436-437.

Skinner, B. F. (1938). *The behavior of organisms: an experimental analysis.* New York: Appleton-Century-Crofts.

Sluckin, W. (1965). *Imprinting and early learning.* Chicago: Aldine Press.

Sluckin, W., Herbert, M., & Sluckin, A. (1983). *Maternal bonding.* Oxford: Basil Blackwell.

Sluckin, W., & Salzen, E. A. (1961). Imprinting and perceptual learning. *Quarterly Journal of Experimental Psychology,* **16,** 65-67.

Solomon, R. L., & Corbit, J. D. (1974). An opponent-process theory of motivation: I. Temporal dynamics of affect. *Psychological Review,* **81,** 119-145.

Van Kampen, H. S., & Bolhuis, J. J. (1991). Auditory learning and filial imprinting in the chick. *Behaviour,* **117,** 303-319.

Waller, P. F., & Waller, M. G. (1963). Some relationships between early experience and later social behavior in ducklings. *Behaviour,* **20,** 343-363.

Index

Index

Index

orphanages 76
oscilloscope 149
overdose 176

P

pain 109–111, 114
pair bonding 170
pane of glass 121–123
Panksepp, J. 96, 133
parent 10, 40, 77, 83, 106, 115–116, 139–140, 156–157, 160
parsimony 162
partial isolates 122–123
parturition 169
Pavlov, I. 46, 80–81, 136
peers 170
Penn State Poultry Farm 6
Pennsylvania State University 6, 51
Penrose, R. v
persistence 25–26
Peterson, N. 9–10, 12, 17–21
pharmacological studies 96
Philadelphia 92
Philosophy club 47–48
photocell 58, 69–70
photograph 56
physical sciences vii
physiological variables 133
Pickering, V.L. 94
pigeon 11, 18–19
pigeon key 14
pip marks 31, 90, 141
placebo 168
plastic milk bottle 12, 14, 25, 37, 45, 58, 130
plastic paddle 13
play activity 100
pleasure 63
poison 111

police vehicles 85
poodle 63
postpartum contact 77–78
preference 115, 162
prepulse inhibition 134, 135
primary motivational condition 93
primary social bond 75, 130, 143
primate 11, 84, 105–106, 118, 140, 167, 169–170, 175
primitive trust 76
Princeton University 151
psychologist 6, 11, 15, 52, 54, 143
psychology 46, 135
punishment 44–46, 57

Q

quadrant 69–71, 73–75
quantum chemistry vi

R

rain forest 167
Rajecki, D.W. 80
Ramsay, A.O. 83
rat 10–11, 47–50, 118, 176
Ratner, A. 68, 72–73, 85, 90, 94, 113–115, 136, 155
receptors 158
recognition 152, 155, 159, 162, 174
redundancy 83
reflex 46, 135
reinforcement 10, 17–21, 37, 39–42, 46–50, 57, 65, 88, 130–132, 137, 142

Index